'Dr. Mary McThomas, in her ground-breaking book, provides a much needed re-examination or re-interpretation of the concept of "citizenship" in the US. By challenging the narrow and restrictive concept of "citizenship" with her "performing citizenship" counter-narrative, she provides us all—scholars, elected officials, residents, etc.—with a more inclusive and just approach of how we treat the most vulnerable among us: undocumented immigrants. Given the rise of xenophobia in this country, not just with Donald Trump but also with his many supporters and like-minded American leaders, those of us who seek justice and dignity for "the other", need to reconsider existing theories and paradigms that perpetuate a system of inequality and exploitation for those who live and work in America's shadows.'

Alvaro Huerta, Ph.D., is an assistant professor of urban and regional planning and ethnic and women's studies at California State Polytechnic University, Pomona. He is the author of *Reframing the Latino Immigration Debate: Towards a Humanistic Paradigm.*

Performing Citizenship

Undocumented migrants in the United States raise compelling questions about political legitimacy, obligation, and citizenship. If they are truly members of their communities, should they have a voice in the laws and policies that impact their lives? Should their interests be considered, especially in light of exploitation by employers, the possibility of detention, and the threat of deportation? This book argues that we do indeed owe certain moral and political obligations to those individuals who have been living and contributing to their communities, regardless of whether they initially arrived without documents. McThomas's argument is based on flipping the way we think about political obligation and state-granted citizenship. Instead of the conventional understanding that the conferral of rights by the state obligates citizens to perform certain duties, she argues that the performance of civic duties and obligations— "performing citizenship"—should trigger corresponding rights and protections. The book combines theory and practice to make this argument, analyzing state-level legislative debates about extending driving privileges and in-state tuition rates to undocumented residents. Consistent with the book's main argument, we see contested notions of what constitutes citizenship in these debates and a growing acknowledgment that those who perform citizenship deserve certain rights and privileges.

Mary McThomas is Assistant Professor of Political Science at California State University, Channel Islands. Her primary research interests include political theories of citizenship, immigration law and politics, the right to privacy, gender and politics, and political ethics.

Performing Citizenship
Undocumented Migrants in
the United States

Mary McThomas

Routledge
Taylor & Francis Group

NEW YORK AND LONDON

First published 2016
by Routledge
711 Third Avenue, New York, NY 10017

and by Routledge
2 Park Square, Milton Park, Abingdon, Oxon, OX14 4RN

First issued in paperback 2018

*Routledge is an imprint of the Taylor & Francis Group,
an informa business*

Library of Congress Cataloging-in-Publication Data
Names: McThomas, Mary, author.
Title: Performing citizenship : undocumented migrants in the
    United States / Mary McThomas.
Description: New York, NY : Routledge, 2016. | Includes bibliographical
    references and index.
Identifiers: LCCN 2016007301 | ISBN 9781138684096 (hbk) |
    ISBN 9781315544175 (ebk)
Subjects: LCSH: Illegal aliens—Government policy—United States. |
    Illegal aliens—Government policy—United States—States. |
    Citizenship—Political aspects—United States. | Illegal aliens—
    Education (Higher)—United States. | Drivers' licenses—United
    States—States.
Classification: LCC JV6483 .M336 2016 | DDC 325.73—dc23
LC record available at http://lccn.loc.gov/2016007301

ISBN 13: 978-1-138-59964-2 (pbk)
ISBN 13: 978-1-138-68409-6 (hbk)

Typeset in Sabon
by Apex CoVantage, LLC

For the next generation: Taylor, Parker, Carson, Chad, Kiefer, Kyra, Jules, and future Tesler children. You inspire me to try to make the world a better—and more just—place.

Contents

Acknowledgments

I am truly grateful for the feedback I received throughout the course of this project. The book benefited greatly by comments from discussants, fellow panelists, and audience members at annual conferences for the American Political Science Association, the Association for Political Theory, and Wayne State University's Center for the Study of Citizenship. I am also extremely thankful to the Political Theory Group at University of California, Irvine, for offering a dedicated and engaged discussion of the project. Special gratitude is due to Els de Graauw, Emily Hallock, and Michael Tesler for thoughtful (and written!) comments on various aspects of the book. In the busy lives we all lead, it is a rare gift to get such thorough and helpful feedback. In addition, I am grateful for assistance provided by my colleagues at California State University, Channel Islands. The fine people of Research and Sponsored Programs provided funding. RSCA (Research, Scholarship, and Creative Activities) Business offered interdisciplinary viewpoints and a supportive sounding board. Finally, Scott Frisch, Department Chair Extraordinaire, helped to protect my time. Last, but certainly not least, I would like to thank Natalja Mortensen, Lillian Rand, and everyone else at Routledge who helped me navigate the publishing process.

1 Introduction

Undocumented migrants in the United States raise some compelling questions about political legitimacy, obligation, and citizenship. If they are truly members of their communities, should they have a voice in the laws and policies that impact their lives? Should their interests be considered, especially in light of exploitation by employers, the possibility of detention, and the threat of deportation? At the same time, though, granting a voice to those who entered the country without nation-state authorization is not without complications, including concerns about the sovereignty of the pre-existing political community. Central to democratic legitimacy and individual autonomy is the ability to know who is author of the laws to which we submit. That is, popular sovereignty rests on the notion that we govern ourselves (even if through representatives) and, in so doing, consent to and legitimate state authority. If we are a government of the people, by the people and for the people, we need to know who constitutes "the people." The fear is that porous borders can change the membership of the political community and therefore alter the "we" that makes up popular sovereignty, leaving existing citizens subject to a new and extended sovereign to which they did not consent. I submit that the role of consent is flawed, the "we" has already changed, and a substantial number of people in the United States are bound by laws that they have no say in creating. Furthermore, without status or standing, they have no hope of being heard or represented in the future.

What I would like to suggest is that we owe a certain moral and political obligation to those individuals who have been living and contributing to their communities, regardless of whether they initially arrived without documents. This is not a theory about migration or borders, but about the migrants themselves who have been living "illegally" within our communities for a sustained amount of time. They have common interests and a shared fate with the rest of the community but are differentiated due to a lack of documents. In making this argument, I call for a shift in the way we conceptualize political obligation and the corollary rights and duties of citizenship.

I argue that migrant nations, such as the United States, where substantial segments of the population have lived within the nation's borders for years without documents, have reached a point where there is a need to reconceptualize traditional notions of what makes a citizen. I make the case to flip the way we think about political obligation and state-granted citizenship. The conventional understanding is that citizens become obligated to the state because the state provides protection and benefits. This obligation requires citizens not only to obey the law, but also to take part in certain civic duties such as paying taxes and contributing in various ways to their communities. By working backwards—by flipping our understandings of political obligation—we can identify activities that satisfy civic duties and obligations and then create corresponding rights. In this formulation, instead of the state's actions triggering obligation on the part of the individual, a person's actions and contributions trigger state protections and benefits.

Citizenship brings with it protections and status as well as certain obligations. If an individual is meeting her obligations as a citizen—what I call "performing citizenship"—should she not have the corresponding rights and protections? I contend that a performance-based conception of citizenship, which focuses on the carrying out of civic duties instead of nation-state authorization, more accurately reflects our current situation and recognizes obligations we have to those living among us. In making this argument, then, the book aims to fundamentally alter the way we think about state-granted citizenship.

Are Obligations Owed to Migrants?

It is often argued that we do not owe anything to those individuals that chose to come here, especially if, in doing so, they violated our federal laws. However, the legal status of migrants is not constant, but varies with political regimes and policy changes. A once-accepted circular flow of people and products among mutually advantaged communities, for instance, becomes "illegal" under a new policy regime. Immigration policies over the last several decades have increasingly criminalized behavior that was once accepted, even encouraged.

There is also a long history of U.S. companies recruiting labor from other countries, especially Mexico, so that the only thing temporary about temporary guest worker programs is the individual worker. The need for and systematic recruitment of "temporary" workers are constant, and recruitment has remained in effect regardless of changing legality. One of the most notable legal recruitments was the Bracero program that resulted from an agreement between the United States and the Mexican government. It began during World War II when the United States was facing labor shortages due to the deployment of able-bodied men and continued until 1964. Over the duration of the program, more than four million Mexican men took part.

The Bracero program ended in large part because of increasing criticism of the American government's failure to protect workers and avoid such workplace abuses as low wages, inadequate housing, and workplace safety. However, when the program ended, companies continued to recruit undocumented workers. Fernandez-Kelly and Massey (2007) have previously written about this change in the legal status of an otherwise unchanged practice. They observe that "after 1965 the United States shifted from a de jure guest worker program based on the circulation of braceros to a de facto guest worker program based on the circulation of undocumented labor" (Fernandez-Kelly and Massey 2007, 107). Merav Lichtenstein similarly recounts the consistent use of temporary labor by U.S. companies. Lichtenstein notes that in the last 10 years, United States employers recruited about 1.5 million immigrant workers, but only allowed visas for one-third of those recruited (Lichtenstein 2007, 703). The remaining two-thirds are still employed, but—without visas—are unauthorized under existing policy. As a result, they are placed in danger of detention and deportation.

The North American Free Trade Agreement (NAFTA) has further exacerbated the issue of increasing demand—both for work and workers—but limiting opportunities to legally migrate and work in the United States. Policies called for by treaty partners (i.e., Canada and the United States)—such as the privatization of Mexican farms—resulted in greater poverty among Mexican citizens. In addition, NAFTA purposely allows for the free movement of products, but not of labor. Instead of granting treaty partners special status, the United States retained pre-NAFTA visa caps for Canadians and Mexicans wishing to come to the United States. As a result, the number of permanent resident visas available to Mexicans is the same as it is for individuals coming from Nepal or Botswana, even though the demand is much higher from Mexican citizens. That surprisingly low level of visas has led Fernandez-Kelly and Massey (2007) to conclude that

> [m]aintaining a quota of twenty thousand visas per year for a nation to which the United States is so closely bound by history, geography, and free trade is unrealistically low, bringing about waiting periods that surpass ten years, creating frustration among qualified applicants, and making it all but certain that illegal migration will continue.
>
> (115)

The wait time has continued to increase, resulting in current estimates of 28–30 years for a Mexican national to legally migrate to the United States. If nothing else, the disproportionate wait time for certain countries problematizes the claim that undocumented individuals living in the United States should just go back to their country of origin and get in line for legal status. Many Americans do not realize how much more difficult it is to legally migrate to the United States today than it was when their ancestors arrived. Consequently, people perceive undocumented residents as taking advantage of the system without knowing current immigration procedure or the larger historical context. While the focus in the above section is on the United States' special relationship with Mexico, it should be noted that recent migrants are much more likely to come from countries other than Mexico, with the greatest increase coming from Asian countries. However, individuals originating from Mexico are still the majority of the settled population in the United States, and it is the settled population that is the focus of this book.

Counter argument often used against providing unauthorized migrants with permanent legal status is that this policy will have a negative effect on the U.S. economy and American workers and harm communities through increases in crime and changes to the national culture. For example, Michael Walzer (1983), in arguing for immigration restriction in order to protect national culture, explains that the

> distinctiveness of cultures and groups depends upon closure and cannot be conceived as a stable feature of human life without it. . . . At some level of political organization something like the sovereign state must take shape and claim the authority

to make its own admission policy, to control and sometimes restrain the flow of immigrants.

(9–10)

Noah Pickus (1998) also warns us that

[r]ights' advocates need to recognize that the current slew of proposals to revalue citizenship by restricting the entry of newcomers and the rights and benefits afforded to immigrants already here are driven not simply by racial and economic fears. These proposals are motivated, in part, by genuine concerns over a loss of sovereignty and common culture and a sense that immigration policy is woefully insulated from public control.

(118)

Underlying these arguments is the idea that it is not that we owe nothing to migrants, it is that we have greater obligations to fellow citizens and our own national culture.

Theoretical arguments voicing legitimate concerns about protecting sovereignty will be discussed in greater detail in the next two chapters. As for obligations to fellow citizens, I find it interesting that some of the scholars who point to concerns about the effect of immigration on disadvantaged citizens are the same scholars who argue that accidents of birth are morally suspect. By accidents of birth, I mean that an individual has no control over where and to what family she is born. One does not work hard to be born into a wealthy family, therefore deserving the extra benefits of wealth; it is merely luck. This raises questions of desert and provides a basis to argue for redistribution programs. The moral concerns surrounding the accidents of birth surely extend beyond class and apply to what nation an individual is born in. Certainly, someone born in the United States, on average, has better life chances than someone born in Haiti. Are United States citizens more deserving, from an ethical standpoint, of better life chances? Similar to being born into a wealthy family, citizens did not work hard to be born in the United States. It was not due to merit, but to luck. As such, what differentiates the baby born in the United States and the baby born in Haiti is not merit or some other morally justifiable distinction; it is countries of origin and the corresponding citizenship. If citizenship is based on a metric other than state-granted documents, as I argue it should be throughout this book, this difference potentially falls away, leaving both children deserving of our considerations.

Larger theoretical issues aside, many opponents of immigrant rights point to economic and social concerns. The related beliefs are that allowing in migrants leads to significant government costs and increased crime rates and results in the lowering of wages and the loss of jobs, specifically hurting the lower classes. A sovereign nation has the right—and the obligation—to protect its own scarce resources and help its own disadvantaged members. Against this backdrop, to help noncitizens is a betrayal. Throughout this book, I will be questioning the metric to determine who is a member of the polity and who is rightfully excluded. That is, if the alien/citizen divide among residents disappears (or does not exist), these concerns do not get the same traction as those undocumented residents performing citizenship would be considered part of the political membership to be considered and protected. Once a part of the "us," spending money on nonnative-born residents is qualitatively different than, for example, a government spending state money on international aid instead of domestic social programs. That being said, there are also reasons to believe that the fears of economic and social costs are overstated.

Daniel Tichenor (2002) provides a historical-institutional analysis of changing immigration policy regimes. One surprising finding was that moves to restrict immigration have occurred during times of prosperity as well as economic recessions. There is more to restrictionist immigration agendas, therefore, than just pocketbook voting or concerns for the U.S. labor force. However, contrary to the fears of many members of the public, studies have shown that unauthorized immigration results in an overall economic gain for the United States. Even groups that call for further restrictions on immigration admit that the net economic effect is positive, but fear that individual states may suffer (e.g., see Borjas 2002). That is, while the federal government benefits from migrants paying federal taxes and unclaimed social security contributions, individual states with larger undocumented resident populations—such as California or New York—will end up paying more than their fair share. States are required to provide primary education to all residents, regardless of legal status, and there are costs resulting from emergency room visits. However, additional state funds allocated to various social programs are entirely voluntary on the part of the state.

In terms of impact on employment, Jeffrey Passel (2011) concludes that immigrants and their children will provide virtually all of the growth in the U.S. labor force over the next 40 years (21). He acknowledges that the growing gap between the aging

U.S. population and younger migrants might lead to a battle for resources, but ultimately concludes that the aging U.S. population is exactly why we need to retain a young workforce to pay into social security (Passel 2011, 26). Such findings led Evelyn Hu-Dehart to claim that immigrants are not only *not* a drain on the U.S. economy, but an absolute necessity (Hu-Dehart 2007, 253). In addition to benefitting economically, it has been shown that the United States reaps social benefits from migration as well. A macro-level, longitudinal study found that increases in immigration actually led to decreases in crime rates in the receiving communities (Ousey and Kubrin 2009).

The above findings speak to the contributions migrants make to our communities—contributions that are not currently recognized. Unfortunately, within our current system, the inability to acknowledge these contributions and recognize the contributors as members of our community has left undocumented residents vulnerable to exploitation by employers and in danger of detention and deportation. Arguments based on human rights or moral obligations have not resulted in the necessary protections. I, therefore, argue that a form of civilly recognized rights are necessary, as voluntary moral obligations have fallen short when it comes to granting respect, consideration, and recognition to undocumented migrants in the United States. Within the framework of liberal democracies, such recognition requires being seen and being heard.

Voice and Recognition in Liberal Democracies

The lack of voice is a crucial factor in our failure to recognize undocumented migrants in the United States. Within the existing liberal framework of Anglo-American law, individuals are defined in terms of how they stand in relation to the state. This is problematic for undocumented migrants and highlights the problem of liberal theory, in which ideas of reciprocity and recognition are strained by noncitizen status. If an individual is not recognized within the system of citizen's rights, they are not heard and often not seen. When operating within a rights-based framework, proponents for the rights of noncitizens attempt to rectify this situation by framing their arguments in terms of human rights. However, such human rights claims have met with limited success. Claims to human rights can be an effective form of moral persuasion but, as with all rights claiming, require a guarantor to ensure the rights being claimed are granted and protected. Barring a global judge, such claims revert to claims against the nation-state, which is especially problematic when the nation-state is the one denying the rights in the first place. Therefore, it is important to move beyond human rights when making claims for the rights of noncitizens.

It has been argued that liberalism has more to do with exit than voice. I would add that it has more to do with exit options than entry options, namely entrance into the political community. The idea that consent is made possible by alternative choices of affiliation is belied by the current reality of state-derived citizenship. Kwame Anthony Appiah (1998) observed that

> [o]nce you begin to think about children and birthright citizenship, it seems to me you have to give up the idea that real consent, of the sort that liberals have imagined—that is, free choice among real options—is really what underlies the citizenship of most citizens anywhere, even in the liberal democracies, today.
>
> (42)

Some might respond by saying that U.S. citizenship can be acquired, thus providing an entry option. However, as discussed above, becoming a citizen of the United States is a long and arduous process limited to only a small percentage of those who wish to be included. While citizenship is only one form of identity and affiliation, it is the main form recognized within a liberal framework of rights and is, therefore, important to those wishing to be heard.

Without citizenship status, an individual is not able to make rights claims or to be recognized. It is as if they do not exist—even though it is widely acknowledged that they are part of our society. Public discourse surrounding the issue of amnesty informatively reveals this tension. On one side, there is an attempt to recognize those who have invested in the United States: working, parenting, and being engaged in their communities. But these discussions reveal the underlying belief that the only answer possible in the liberal state is through citizenship. An individual cannot be recognized without bearing citizen's rights. The phrase consistently used in tandem with a "path to citizenship" is "coming out of the shadows"—as if these individuals do not exist prior to political recognition. Liberal theory—and the resulting liberal state—is constructed in such a way that we are unable to recognize humans living and working in our communities because they do not bear the stamp and voice of a citizen.

The linkage between being heard and being recognized has been explored by deliberative democratic theorists, who have discussed the importance of creating a space and opportunity for people to deliberate and have drawn attention to the potentially political and subject-creating act of speech. However, theorists have also pointed to issues of access to—and power differentials within—arenas of public discourse (Benhabib 1996, Button and Mattson 1999, and Young 2001). Critics have brought to light several concerns that call into question the supposedly inclusive and democratic nature of the deliberative process. Such concerns include the privileging of rational debate over other forms of communication; the potential impact of social and economic status and levels of education on the ability—as well as the confidence—to take part in deliberations; and the practice of excluding altogether certain topics from deliberations, as those with the power to set the agenda limit the subject matter.

However, even with the acknowledgment of power asymmetries and the proposed correctives, deliberative theories fall short of providing an inclusive and safe space for democratic discourse. The limitations of such theories are especially stark when extended to a population that is vulnerable to deportation once they speak openly. In this situation, their vulnerability is directly linked to their recognition; the moment they give voice to their true identity and interests, they have opened themselves up to legal sanctions. Further protections are necessary before such an open discourse can occur. In the case of undocumented migrants, having the protections and status that some level of citizenship would impart would go a long way in mitigating these concerns. Without such protections, deliberative theorists have very little to say to undocumented migrants about being heard.

One option often discussed as a way to realize a happy medium between amnesty and deportation is granting more worker visas. This compromise position is an acknowledgment of those individuals already working and contributing to society through their labor and potentially provides a form of recognition. It also acknowledges that actions, such as businesses recruiting undocumented workers, may trigger obligations on the part of the United States to recognize these workers and protect them from deportation. However, worker visas do not provide much more protection than that, as they do not grant rights and are tied to a single employer. This latter condition prohibits the visa bearer from switching jobs, which undermines any ability to seek more competitive wages or better conditions. In addition, visas tied to one employer results in even greater power differentials between employer and employee, as the worker serves at the whim of her boss who can send her home if she is no longer needed or wanted. Even if the policy was amended to allow the visa to be attached to the employee instead of the employer, critics are concerned that workplace abuses would continue. This concern is well grounded, given the long history of workers being exploited while in the United States on temporary visas. Others have raised concerns that increasing worker visas would create a permanent class of subcitizens. Thus, the supposed happy medium between citizen and deportee would really just be, at best, a second-class citizen. At worst, the workers would be seen as a separate—and disposable—class, providing cheap labor at the whim of the company and the state.

Along with those practical concerns, there is also the more theoretical issue of using worker visas as the road to recognition and reciprocity. Holding a worker visa means you are recognized through the market. This may undermine or discount your non-economic contributions to your community. Michael Ignatieff in "The Myth of Citizenship" provides what he sees as two conflicting images between political and market citizenship. He explains that

> one defends a political, the other an economic definition of man, the one an active—participatory—conception of freedom, the other a passive—acquisitive—definition of freedom; the one speaks of society as a polis; the other of society as a market-based association of competitive individuals.
>
> (Ignatieff 1995, 54)

Market-based man may be a mode of citizenship recognized in the modern liberal community, but it is inadequate for the acknowledgement of community membership I am proposing here and a potential consequence of relying on worker visas as a form of recognition.

I suggest, instead, that the situation requires us to move beyond the limitations of rights claiming and ethical theories of obligation and move toward creating a new conception of citizenship with its corollary protections. While modern liberalism fails to extend moral commitments to undocumented migrants living in our communities, ethical theories of moral obligation fail to provide the level of legal protection granted by liberal citizenship. An understanding of citizenship as a shared common life can be expanded upon to derive a performance-based conception of citizenship that is based on shared experiences and communal obligations. I argue that there is a possibility of genuine recognition, reciprocity among group members, and a voice for all that have a shared fate with that group, regardless of whether an individual group member is a properly documented, rights-bearing citizen in the liberal schema.

If some form of political citizenship is the best (if not only) way for an individual to be recognized and heard and have a voice in the laws to which she submits, it is necessary to further explore the basis for inclusion into—and exclusion from—this category. As with most concepts, there is a danger of believing that the current situation is somehow natural; that is, it has been and always will be this way. As discussed above, the history of immigration policy in the United States reflects an ever-changing idea about migration and migrants. An individual is "illegal" because current policy has deemed them so. This has changed through the years depending on politics, business interests, and public opinion, as well as on evolving conceptions of citizenship. Therefore, it can change again.

Current Constructions of Citizenship

I explore existing theories of citizenship in greater detail in the next chapter. But it is important to note that scholars have questioned constructions of citizenship as well as the myths surrounding the creation and sustenance of the nation-state, including whether it is both nation and state. That is, do the cultural and historical connections of a people (nation) correspond to political boundaries (state)? This is important as we question whether nation-state authorization is a necessary component of citizenship. Anthony Marx questions the accounts that suggest nations arose as a social process of solidarity; thus a natural, cohesive, and voluntary political community.

> The result has been described by Benedict Anderson as an "imagined community," by Homi Bhabha as a common "narration," by Deutsch as "communication," and by Habermas as solidarity and legitimation based on a consensus made possible by common language. These arguments share with the liberal tradition the assumption that early social/national cohesion requires no institutional action; there is no state action necessary to encourage the process of community cohesion or loyalty.
>
> (Marx 2003, 15)

Marx claims that for such cohesive communities to coincide with political boundaries, there must be a political process to create nation-state communities. That is, such social groupings cannot magically correspond with political institutions unless there was a political process at play. In reality, and counter to national myths, cohesive political communities—with shared interests and fates—exist within nation-states as well as across state lines. Thus, affinity, allegiance, and obligation to one's group is based on more than politically constructed lines on a map. This suggests that we must look elsewhere for a reason to claim the nation-state as exceptional and deserving of our moral and political obligations.

It is helpful to re-examine existing theories of citizenship in order to explore this issue and the relationship between political communities and their members. To that end, in Chapter Two, I provide an overview of theories of citizenship and discuss their contributions and limitations in terms of recognizing undocumented members of our communities. I then proceed in Chapter Three to discuss theories of political obligation and my own argument to flip our traditional understandings as a first step towards extending rights and protections to those not currently recognized by the state. I argue that instead of using a top-down approach in which we owe duties to the state because it protects us, we should use a bottom-up approach in which the performance of citizen-like duties trigger the state's protections. The question then becomes, what counts as citizen-like duties? Chapter Three attempts to answer this question from a theoretical approach by using the duties and special obligations discussed in the political obligation literature to create a new metric to determine who should be included in the political community.

After putting forth those theoretical arguments, Chapters Four and Five analyze debates regarding state-level policies to reveal underlying—and shifting—constructions of citizenship.

State and local governments in the United States are increasingly acknowledging that their membership might include more than those recognized by the federal government and that, as a result, undocumented residents should be granted certain benefits. To explore this further, I look at state legislation that extends privileges to undocumented members of the community. I focus on two main policy areas. Chapter Four concentrates on state-based DREAM Acts that allow undocumented students to benefit from in-state tuition rates. In Chapter Five, I focus on the extension of driving privileges to undocumented state residents. In both cases, I track the arguments used for and against these policies to uncover conceptions of citizenship and notions of community used to frame, justify, or oppose the policies. In looking at the debates, there is a clear divide between those who rely solely on nation-state status and those who want to take other actions and characteristics into account when determining who is deserving of state benefits. What is also present is the growing contestation of older notions of citizenship and a call to reconfigure requirements for inclusion.

The analyses in the chapters that follow suggest that it is important to retain the protections granted by citizenship, as our mere moral obligations have proven to be insufficient for the humane treatment of the undocumented migrants living in our communities. Calls to human rights and global citizenship have proven to be too distant a concept to help on the ground. A flipped understanding of political obligation resulting in performance-based citizenship could more accurately reflect real life and more readily provide protections than superordinate structures such as the United Nations. In addition, performance-based citizenship would reflect the human side of the individual. Instead of the truncated vision of a temporary worker constructed by proponents of worker visas, it allows for a fuller depiction and recognition of members of our community engaged in a variety of human activities.

At a minimum, flipping our understanding of political obligation would lead to the acknowledgement of the contribution undocumented members are already making to our communities, even though they do not get the benefits granted by the state. Furthermore, a performance-based conception of citizenship would obligate us to treat those within our communities with the respect and humanity deserving of free and equal persons within our polity. We cannot continue to pretend that the undocumented individual is invisible. They are not living in the "shadows" because they are hiding—they work, study, and live with us—but because we fail to recognize them. Charles Taylor (1994) argues that the recognition of persons, in their distinct cultural identities, is essential to our very characteristics as human beings. Taylor was talking about recognition of group identities of minority groups, not noncitizens. However, our current situation requires the same level of recognition. To do less dehumanizes and undermines self-respect. To do more opens up the potential for a flourishing, diverse, committed community.

References

Appiah, Kwame Anthony. 1998. "Citizenship in Theory and Practice: A Response to Charles Kesler." In *Immigration and Citizenship in the Twenty-First Century*, edited by Noah M. J. Pickus, 41–47. Lanham: Rowman & Littlefield Publishers, Inc.

Benhabib, Seyla. 1996. "Toward a Deliberative Model of Democratic Legitimacy." In *Democracy and Difference: Contesting the Boundaries of the Political*, edited by Seyla Benhabib, 67–94. Princeton: Princeton University Press.

Borjas, George J. 2002. "Welfare Reform and Immigrant Participation in Welfare Programs." *International Migration Review*, Vol. 36, No. 4 (Winter), 1093–1123.

Button, Mark and Kevin Mattson. 1999. "Deliberative Democracy in Practice: Challenges and Prospects for Civic Deliberation." *Polity*, Vol. 31, No. 4 (Summer), 609–637.

Fernandez-Kelly, Patricia and Douglas S. Massey. 2007. "Borders for Whom? The Role of NAFTA in Mexico-U.S. Migration." *Annals of the American Academy of Political and Social Science*, Vol. 610, No. 1 (March), 98–118.

Hu-Dehart, Evelyn. 2007. "Globalization and Its Discontents: Exposing the Underside." In *Gender on the Borderlands*. Lincoln: University of Nebraska Press.

Ignatieff, Michael. 1995. "The Myth of Citizenship." In *Theorizing Citizenship*, edited by Ronald Beiner, 53–77. Albany: State University of New York Press.

Lichtenstein, Merav. 2007. "An Examination of Guest Worker Reform Policies in the United States." *Cardozo Public Law, Policy & Ethics Journal*, Vol. 5, No. 3 (Spring), 689–727.

Marx, Anthony W. 2003. *Faith in Nation: Exclusionary Origins of Nationalism*. New York: Oxford University Press.

Ousey, Graham C. and Charis E. Kubrin. 2009. "Exploring the Connection between Immigration and Violent Crime Rates in U.S. Cities, 1980–2000." *Social Problems*, Vol. 56, No. 3 (August), 447–473.

Passel, Jeffrey S. 2011. "Demography of Immigrant Youth: Past, Present, and Future." *The Future of Children*, Vol. 21, No. 1 (Spring), 19–41.

Pickus, Noah. 1998. "To Make Natural: Creating Citizens for the Twenty-First Century." In *Immigration and Citizenship in the Twenty-First Century*, edited by Noah M. J. Pickus, 107–139. Lanham: Rowman & Littlefield Publishers, Inc.

Taylor, Charles. 1994. "The Politics of Recognition." In *Multiculturalism: Examining the Politics of Recognition*, edited by Amy Gutmann, 25–74. Princeton: Princeton University Press.

Tichenor, Daniel J. 2002. *Dividing Lines: The Politics of Immigration Control in America*. Princeton: Princeton University Press.

Young, Iris Marion. 2001. "Activist Challenges to Deliberative Democracy." *Political Theory*, Vol. 29, No. 5 (October), 670–690.

2 The Limitations of Existing Theories of Citizenship

Migration patterns, transnational identities, and transborder relationships have led some to question previously held conceptions of the nation-state. Nation-state borders and individual identities based on singular citizenship are increasingly seen as constructed fictions. Many theorists question the Westphalian notion of citizenship in which loyalty to one territorially based nation-state is seen as exclusive, necessary, and sufficient. However, this questioning tends to lead to either a cosmopolitan vision of global citizenship or a group identity-based notion of differentiated citizenship. By my account, though, both fail to address the concerns raised by individuals living "illegally" within a national polity.

Modern liberalism remains the hegemonic theory of both state and citizen in the United States. Yet modern liberalism, with its focus on individual *qua* citizen, fails to extend moral commitments to undocumented migrants living in our communities. Conversely, ethical theories of moral obligation fail to provide the level of legal protection granted by liberal citizenship. Thus, a new conception of citizenship is necessary to both recognize our obligations to members of our community and to provide them protection and voice within the polity. In this chapter, I will discuss existing theories of citizenship and explore what they offer—and what they fail to provide—in terms of this quest for a more inclusive understanding of political membership. I then introduce my argument for a performance-based conception of citizenship.

The Liberal Model of Citizenship

Liberal theory, while multifaceted and contested, broadly claims that individuals are free and equal beings—the bearers of fundamental rights that cannot be infringed upon by the state. Liberal citizenship is largely rights-based, with the state envisioned as a neutral arbiter and guarantor of individual rights. In both liberal theory and liberal democracies, recognition occurs by and through the state. Within this framework, undocumented migrants are defined in terms of how they stand in relation to the state, hence the strange conception of an individual herself being "illegal," as opposed to an individual committing an illegal act. Because liberal theory is based on the individual *qua* citizen instead of individual *qua* human, it is unable to accommodate the reality of individuals living within our communities without the authorization by—and recognition of—the nation-state.

There have been many criticisms of liberal theory, especially the formulation of the individual as an atomistic rights-bearer with no ties, obligations, or pre-existing conditions. These critiques have exposed the limits of liberalism in confronting gender inequalities and domestic hierarchies (e.g., see Okin 1987, Pateman 1988, and Young 1990) as well as structural racism (e.g., see Mills 1999 and Pateman and Mills 2007); failing to take account of both the effects and benefits of the community within which the individual rights-bearer exists (e.g., see Sandel 1982, 1984, and 1990; MacIntyre, Kommers, and Solomon 1990, Glendon 1991, and Etzioni 1996a and 1996b); and the related criticism of not recognizing cultural membership as a "primary good" (e.g., see Kymlicka 1989 and 1995, and Taylor 1994). Those who lack citizenship status are yet another group that modern liberalism has rendered invisible.

Modern liberalism rests heavily upon the shoulders of John Rawls, and we see many of his arguments treated as basic premises in later works. As such, I treat Rawls's work in greater depth than that of the other authors discussed below. In his *Theory of Justice* (1971) and subsequent reiterations and explanations, Rawls created a brilliant vision of a political conception of justice. One of the many features of his multifaceted theory is a focus on the least advantaged of society and a reasoned argument why justice requires that they *should* be considered. His idea of the veil of ignorance, in which individuals do not know their identity (class, race, gender, generation, etc.), seems especially promising in addressing issues of justice for those who lack legal status in a society. However, while he argues for a public conception of justice, it is one intended for and shared by citizens.[1] Rawls specifies that "the parties in the original position" act "as citizens' representatives" (Rawls 1985, 238). Even when participants put aside all markers and knowledge of identity, they are still citizens. That is the sole enduring characteristic that is present under the veil of ignorance. While apropos for a political theory of the state, this focus on citizens undermines the ability to extend equal consideration to noncitizens within the state.[2]

To be fair, Rawls explicitly bounds his theory by stating it is for a closed society, entered into only by birth and exited only through death. It is reasonable and perhaps even necessary to focus solely on citizens while creating and justifying a political conception of justice (at least using the current time-slice approach). But within the liberal framework, it is as if noncitizens cease to exist. It is only the voice of citizens who are recognized within political society through rights claiming.

In specifically addressing immigration, Rawls writes

> that an important role of government, however arbitrary a society's boundaries may appear from a historical point of view, is to be the effective agent of a people as they take responsibility for their territory and the size of their population, as well as for maintaining the land's environmental integrity.
>
> (Rawls 1999, 8)

Rawls never clarifies why future generations are to be considered, while future citizens via migration are explicitly excluded from consideration. A clue to this distinction may be his belief that one "reason for limiting immigration is to protect a people's political culture and its constitutional principles" (Rawls 1999, 39 fn 48). In this we see the idea that individuals born into the nation-state will be properly educated in the shared beliefs of the society as they mature, whereas individuals that arrive already fully formed may not be properly inculcated and formed in such a way as to maintain the well-ordered society.[3] If we accept Rawls's qualifications, then we accept that it is reasonable and perhaps even necessary to focus solely on citizens while creating and justifying a political conception of justice. After all, undocumented migrants have no political claims against the state in which they now reside. It is only the voice of citizens who are recognized within political society through rights claiming.

Rawls argues that his form of political liberalism is a credible basis for social unity, as even those who hold different comprehensive doctrines can agree on a singular political conception of justice. He concludes "that this provides a sufficient as well as the most reasonable basis of social unity available to us as citizens of a democratic society" (Rawls 2001, 9). While Rawls never loses his focus on citizens and the political nature of his theory, he does have some slippage when he starts talking about social unity in this way. There is a presumption that social unity is found through and based on citizenship. It denies other forms of connection, commonly held beliefs, and shared experiences. However, Rawls makes clear that he is writing a political theory, not a moral theory; his stated attempt is to be political, not metaphysical. In this case, the bounded subject is the individual *qua* citizen, and the virtues in question are limited to political virtues of citizenship. So while Rawls argues for "[f]reedom of movement and free choice of occupation," such rights are not extended outside of the political community (Rawls 2001, 58). The promise of liberalism, therefore, holds no hope for the noncitizen.

Rawls's focus on citizens misses the sad truth that undocumented individuals are often one of the least advantaged and most exploited groups within our borders. Their undocumented status leaves them vulnerable to the abuse of others and in greater need of protection. Rawls describes the least advantaged as

> not, if all goes well, the unfortunate and unlucky—objects of our charity and compassion, much less our pity—but those to whom reciprocity is owed as a matter of political justice among those who are free and equal citizens along with everyone else.
> (Rawls 2001, 139)

He does not offer an explanation as to why reciprocity is only owed to citizens. Why do connections to the nation-state matter more than any other connection? Is it institutional convenience? Or do we believe we will only have true reciprocity with someone who is as equally bound to political obligations as we are? If this is the case, perhaps we should reconsider the reciprocity and recognition owed to those who are engaged in our communities and share in our common goals and fates, regardless of their relationship to the larger nation-state. That is, if they are equally bound by civic obligations, perhaps we owe them more than is currently thought. That would, however, require a shift away from state-granted citizenship and political rights limited by citizenship status. One such attempt to move beyond loyalties bounded by borders and limited rights is cosmopolitan theories of citizenship.

Cosmopolitanism: Citizens of the World

Cosmopolitanism addresses the deficits of liberal theory and holds much promise for the concerns of noncitizens. There are different shades of cosmopolitanism but with a similar call to go beyond nation-state borders and reconceptualize our obligations and connections within a global framework. The cosmopolitan claim that an individual can be a citizen of the world potentially allows for broader recognition and acceptance and greater opportunity for mobility. If you are a citizen of the world you should be welcome anywhere, thus allowing for the mobility necessary to find employment and reunite with family. More importantly, cosmopolitans—by shifting the focus beyond the bounded nation-state to the global community—move away from the limitations of state-granted political rights and focus instead on human rights. Consequently, each individual—as a human—deserves equal consideration, respect, and basic human rights (e.g., see Heater 2002, Kingsbury 2007, and Gaige 2008). Human rights adhere to the individual regardless of the nation-state in which the individual resides and in spite of how she might have come to reside there. Thus, ideally, all individuals have the ability to make claims to certain protections and entitlements on the basis of their humanity.

The shift from citizen's rights to human rights also expands the community to whom is owed certain considerations. As Linda Bosniak (2000) notes, the phrase world citizen "is shorthand for a cosmopolitan outlook that expresses loyalty and moral commitment to humanity at large, rather than any particular community of persons" (448). If human rights are taken seriously and given more attention than (or even equal to) citizen rights, the parochial privileging of citizen over noncitizen is no longer justified. In addition, a cosmopolitan conception of citizenship extends political notions of justice. Seyla Benhabib discusses the shift from national and international justice, predicated on positive laws and treaties, to cosmopolitan norms of justice that "accrue to individuals as moral and legal persons in a worldwide civil society" (Benhabib 2006, 16). Nation-states decline in importance as individual actors take the stage. Instead of nations making agreements with each other on the part of their people, all humans are engaged in the project of justice.

A cosmopolitan vision has clear advantages for undocumented residents, as their human rights claims would be recognized in a way that currently does not happen under liberal theory and the resulting liberal democracies. In addition, the community would owe undocumented residents equal consideration. However, certain limitations of cosmopolitanism make it difficult for this vision to be realized. Critics of cosmopolitanism point to the difficulty in identifying and protecting human rights; the lack—and impracticality—of institutional structures leading to an unacknowledged reliance on the nation-state; and the threat of undermining state sovereignty.

Identifying and agreeing on human rights is not without conflict. Beyond very basic rights of survival, there is much disagreement about what should be included and protected. This is true within a nation, but even more so among nations and cultures. This issue drew notable attention during the United Nations–sponsored 1993 World Conference on Human Rights, which brought together most countries with the intent of developing a declaration of international human rights. Prior to the conference, several Asian countries met and issued the Bangkok Declaration, voicing their concerns that human rights were a Western construct in need of a more pluralistic viewpoint (Amstutz 2013, 101–102). Even if certain universal rights are identified and agreed upon, human rights lack any sort of credible guarantor. Without a global power willing and able to enforce human rights claims, adjudication and enforcement reverts to the nation-state. Benhabib acknowledges this dilemma when she writes that "Cosmopolitan right trumps positive law, although there is no higher sovereign authority that is authorized to enforce it" (Benhabib 2006, 26). Thus, a state is necessary to protect even those rights deemed universal. This leads to a related concern that the institutional structures necessary for cosmopolitanism do not exist and are impractical, leading to a continued reliance on the nation-state.

David Hollinger (1998) observes, "'Citizens of the world' rightly pride themselves on being able to see beyond the parochialism and prejudices of tribe or nation, but they have always had a hard time finding institutional structures and political constituencies to advance their cause" (85). Our current international situation still consists of a constellation of nation-states. To move beyond this and to transition from states as actors to individuals within a larger global network would require some form of global governance. Yet, a global government with real enforcement capability is problematic. To whom would this global government (and police power) be accountable?

In drawing a distinction between cosmopolitanism's global citizen and a globally oriented citizen, Bhiku Parekh argues that the "cosmos is not yet a *polis*, and we should not even try to make it one by creating a world state, which is bound to be remote, bureaucratic, oppressive and culturally bland. If global citizenship means being a citizen of the world, it is neither practicable nor desirable" (Parekh 2003, 12). In this, we see not only the claim that global structures are impractical, but also a related concern that cosmopolitanism suffers from the same anemic set of commitments and obligations for which liberalism is criticized. If our commitments to a national population are potentially strained because the community is too large to care about and the overlapping consensus too thin, the commitment at the international level would be strained to the point of rupture. It is very hard to care for everyone in the world in any more than a superficial way over a sustained amount of time. Strong allegiances and communal commitments require a more individual level of connection based on family ties, personal obligations, and care.

Finally, cosmopolitanism is accused of threatening state sovereignty. It should be noted that many theories attempting to denationalize citizenship are similarly accused, and my theory certainly falls within that camp. Potentially undermining sovereignty is a serious concern. Nation-states have boundaries and, while increasingly porous, they still represent a specific polis and community of members. As one scholar concludes, "[t]o say that no human is illegal is to call into question the entire architecture of sovereignty" (Nyers 2003, 1089). This does not just speak to the state's decision of whom to include and exclude, but also to the legitimated authority that rests in the body of the citizenry. Benhabib notes this problem as follows:

> Such conflicts render starkly visible the "paradox of democratic legitimacy," namely, the necessary and inevitable limitation of democratic forms of representation and accountability in terms of the formal distinction between members and nonmembers. This is the core tension, even if not contradiction, between democratic self-determination and the norms of cosmopolitan justice.
>
> (Benhabib 2006, 17)

As Benhabib points out, though, this is problematic when the very nature of such membership norms leads to the excluded not being party to the discussions regarding the rules of their exclusion. Once again, we find ourselves facing the issue of recognition and voice. Given this situation, she suggests what she calls a "jurisgenerative process," in which the public reconstitutes itself through discussions of inclusion and exclusion, and democratic iterations, in which voice is extended to those who are publicly present regardless of their status. While a hopeful vision, this is still reminiscent of the asymmetries in deliberative democracy in which the excluded require an emissary to voice their claims.

Bonnie Honig argues for a democratic, denationalizing cosmopolitanism that focuses on a more local level and shifts citizenship from a legal status to an activity (Honig 1997a and 2003). She argues that

> democratic principles are best realized . . . in a commitment to a politically engaged, democratic cosmopolitanism in which the will to national unity or identity is attenuated and democratic actors have room to seek out political, cultural, and other forms of not just identity-based affiliation at the subnational, national and international registers. Increasingly, democratic practice exceeds the states it seems to presuppose: democracy's demos is dispersed.
>
> (Honig 1997b, 113)

It is this idea of a dispersed democratic demos based on the practice of democracy that I expand upon in the book. If my conception of performing citizenship were taken into account, the noncitizen would be recognized as an equal member of the community. Such recognition is impossible under the political conception of justice underlying rights-based liberalism precisely because liberal theory is limited by its formulation of individual *qua* citizen.

In her discussion of the tension between democratic legitimacy and cosmopolitan norms, Benhabib concludes that "[p]olitical actors need bounded communities—whether they be cities, regions, states or transnational institutions—within which they can establish mechanisms of representation, accountability, participation and deliberation" (Benhabib 2006, 169). In this understanding, a bounded political community may be necessary for democratic legitimacy and self-determination, but that community is not synonymous with the nation-state. As Bosniak (2000) argues,

> it should not be necessary, it seems to me, to establish precisely where the outer boundaries lie in order to plausibly argue that at least *some* politically and socially-based non-state

communities—including some that have taken form across national boundaries—can serve as sites of citizenship identity and solidarity.

(488)

She goes on to write that there

> are good reasons, grounded in commitments to social justice and democratic engagement, to challenge the presumed inevitability and desirability of a statist conception of citizenship and to prefer, instead, a multiple, pluralized understanding of citizenship identities and solidarities (however uncertain the precise institutional forms these might take may be).
>
> (Bosniak 2000, 508)

Normative theories are not always practical or given to precise policies. Even so, it is important to question the status quo, interrogate our current conceptions and practices, and imagine a more just world.

If we are not reliant on the nation-state for granting political status, a new set of issues (and opportunities) arise. If members of the community are to be autonomous authors of their own laws, we must have good and weighty reasons to justify the exclusion of any of those voices. Documents granted (or not) by the larger nation-state may not be a necessary or sufficient condition for inclusion or exclusion. I argue that a performance-based citizenship—*performing citizenship*—is a way of creating a bounded political community that more accurately reflects communities in the United States and recognizes the obligations and duties that are carried out by those we currently exclude from consideration. What needs to be determined, however, is the nature of the bounded polity (i.e., is it limited to communities or cities?) and what activities count as performing citizenship. In order to think through these issues, I will now turn to civic republicanism for a more duty-based form of citizenship followed by an exploration of the possibility of citizenship granted by smaller polities through ideas of communitarianism and urban citizenship.

Civic Republicanism

Rights-based liberal citizenship can be described as a vertical relationship between sovereign and subject, whereas a republican form of citizenship reflects a more horizontal relationship among citizens. In this latter formulation, importance is placed on each individual's obligation to fellow citizens and duties carried out through various forms of civic and political engagement. This more duty-based framework, adopted by civic republicans, offers an alternative to liberal theories of citizenship and provides another way of justifying the special status of citizen. It also shifts the focus away from citizens' obligations to the state to their obligations to each other. Thus, in civic republicanism, there is more of a sense of communal obligation and shared responsibility that requires a commitment to fellow compatriots.

Civic republicans respond to the anemic, supposedly neutral ties of liberal citizenship with a robust version of commitment and belonging. Proponents envision a much more internalized, core emotional attachment to the state than the neutral and reasoned connection between a citizen and the liberal state apparatus. As Gaige (2008) explains,

> Republicanism reaches past liberalism's near-totalizing emphasis on individual rights by obliging citizens to play active roles in their own respective communities (however defined), as well as in politics and government (at whatever levels). In the eyes of its supporters, it gives life to liberalism and repositions it toward a higher level of engagement in a far more significant sphere, the community.
>
> (127)

While seemingly welcoming engagement at all levels and in all forms, civic republicans still focus on citizens and the nation-state, leading some to interpret the strong emotional attachments described as a version of patriotism.

Noah Pickus, in his arguments for civic nationalism, describe this type of communal engagement that is ultimately tied to the nation-state project. He claims that

> America needs citizens who feel an emotional attachment to the nation, who are committed to the principles of the constitution, and who are willing to engage in the constant political work it will take to balance that attachment and commitment. It needs civic nationalists.
>
> (Pickus 2005, 184)

One of the ways of encouraging civic nationalism among foreign-born residents, according to Pickus, is through an involved process of naturalization.

> In the absence of strong institutional mechanisms for incorporating newcomers into American life, the naturalization process could help forge a communal sense of obligation. This mutual commitment then would derive from an emotional attachment to a shared identity as well as an abstract set of principles. It will issue, in part, from a sense of shared history and fate.
>
> (Pickus 1998, 125)

I agree that a sense of shared history and fate is important in creating communal bonds, and I grant that perhaps the naturalization process is one vehicle of encouraging such attachments. However, I submit that such feelings already exist among individuals living in our communities; individuals unable to go through the naturalization process because they are unauthorized and cannot adjust their legal status under existing immigration laws. Thus, additional mechanisms are required to acknowledge the civic nationalists who already exist but are not recognized.

Another difference between horizontal and vertical frameworks of citizenship is the role of recognition. Whereas vertical models of citizenship concentrate on recognition from the state, horizontal structures call for recognition and reciprocity from other community members. This reciprocity ideally includes mutual respect, equal consideration, and an acknowledgment of a certain level of interdependence. Adrian Oldfield views citizens as autonomous agents, but calls attention to the fact that each individual citizen stands in a relationship of mutual dependence with other citizens (Oldfield 1990, 41). However, this relationship of interdependence between citizens and those without nation-state authorization is masked. The citizens of the United States depend on the labor and taxes paid by migrants, but the legal vulnerability of undocumented residents gives the appearance that they are wholly dependent on the mercy of native citizens. This unequal status undermines the recognition of ongoing relationships in which the ties of interdependence continue to strengthen. This blindness is one of the results of focusing on legal status over civic engagement and contribution.

Civic republicanism—properly understood—is still crucially linked to the nation-state. For this reason, adjustments to civic republican theories and formulations are necessary in order to transcend nationally granted citizenship. For example, if we were to adopt a more localized vision that allows for a focus on the community—whatever that community may be—we may be able to reap the benefits of civic republicanism without the current prerequisite of state-granted citizenship.

Communitarianism

Civic republicanism and communitarianism have many similarities. However, communitarians, sometimes self-identified as modern civic republicans, move away from the vision of the state as community in which citizens are connected to the state through affect-laden ties of love and obligation. Instead, they focus on those voluntary allegiances that occur at a smaller level of association. They introduce the "third realm" of community (friends, neighbors, voluntary associations) into the traditional liberal standoff between the state and individual.

There is very little role for the community in liberal theory. If anything, it is something that the individual has to overcome in order to be truly neutral—a private set of associations that is chosen after the individual is fully developed, not one in which the individual is bred. These voluntary associations may reflect the private beliefs of the individual, but can be bracketed and held apart from the political conception of justice. In contrast, communitarians view membership in a community (be that national, local, ethnic, religious, or associational) as a source of one's identity—not something that can be bracketed—and crucial to creating a stronger connection and deeper loyalty among group members. In turn, this sense of belonging and loyalty inspires a willingness to sacrifice and work for the good of that community in a way that liberalism's welfare state requires, yet fails to do.

In addition to offering a sense of belonging in a way that the neutral state cannot, connections to the community help to shape identity and character. In fact, communal forces can take the place of state-run social controls, such as the police force. Communitarians argue that, when properly developed, a strong community can lead to less police involvement, as the community's use of censure and encouragement replace the need for formal enforcement of laws. Their argument is that the more you allow for community scrutiny, the less you need state control. Communal forces can foster prosocial behavior, replacing the need for invasive laws and regulations.

This belief in the ability of communal forces to shape behavior relies on the idea that the members of a more localized community know each other on a broader (and deeper) range of characteristics than a bureaucratic state can. This is potentially beneficial for undocumented members of the community. The ability to recognize the person on a deeper level than legal status allows community policing in terms of who is committing crimes; that is, the community is able to determine which individuals are committing illegal acts, not who *is* "illegal."

There are, however, concerns with this model, too. First of all, such community policing as described above can be troublesome. There is a rather ominous nature to it, in that your neighbors have the ability and often the interest to pay closer attention to your actions than "big brother" ever would. Such community pressure is also insidious in that it can be internalized. Illiberal communities can foster prejudice and suffocate alternative life choices. There is also the fear of regional bias and potential exploitation. The iron cage of the bureaucracy, if nothing else, is faceless and impartial. That is, it is exactly the neutral apparatus of the state criticized by communitarians and civil republicans as a mere "procedural republic" that (ideally) ensures unbiased decision-making. Localism has the potential to breed particularism and prejudice if new members are viewed with suspicion for being somehow unlike the existing community. If the community can decide to accept you, they can also opt to exclude you for not disinterested reasons.

This problem of biased exclusion also speaks to concerns about insular groups and the need to link community-based citizenship with local governance, so that the "communities" are not a matter of self-selected groups. Ronald Beiner (1995) suggests that it is dangerous if different groups each withdraw "behind the boundaries of its own groupist identity, with no need to acknowledge a larger common culture. Citizenship would then be reduced to an aggregate of subnational ghettoes" (6). This is linked to concerns that encouraging a commitment to subcommunities may undermine national commitments, especially if the priority of national citizenship is downgraded as a source of connection and obligation. Attachment to one's subcommunity can lead to parochialism as an individual privileges her in-group over the rest of the nation. Such parochialism would constrict, not expand, our obligations to others.

That being said, the duty-based nature of communitarian citizenship provides important insights into the issue of whom to include into the polis. If an individual is fulfilling her duties, perhaps that is enough to allow her the reciprocal right to take part in the political decision-making of her community. Additionally, communitarianism asks us to question who should be the gatekeeper of our communities: the nation-state or some more local body? These ideas are picked up and further articulated by proponents of urban citizenship.

Urban Citizenship

Urban citizenship attempts to decouple nation-state status from local citizenship by focusing on a "right to the city" that is premised on a sense of place and belonging rather than formal recognition by the federal government. An individual's physical presence in a polity is the "proof" of residency and "[m]embership would be treated as a matter of social fact rather than legal status" (Nyers 2010, 137). Tony Roshan Samar describes how urban citizenship offers something that liberal models of citizenship cannot by shifting the focus away from individual rights-bearers toward social networks among fellow city residents.

> The liberal democratic model of citizenship revolves around an abstract individual in whom certain political rights, inalienable or otherwise, are vested. . . . In response, "right to the city" offers a broader, socially grounded vision of rights, one in which the social spaces and social networks that underpin the political power of urban populations are protected with at least the same force as the political rights of the individual.
>
> (Roshan Samar 2012, 47)

Urban citizenship provides a wonderful vision of community-based membership and extends our understandings of who should count as citizens of the polis, as well as what polis should be considered (i.e., city, state, or nation). There are real, practical results with the application of this theory, as we have witnessed with the creation of sanctuary cities and certain localities that offer municipal ID cards as a way to reflect that an individual belongs in the city—is, in fact, documented by the city—regardless of nation-state immigration status. However, these policies are restricted to certain cities, which in turn leads to some limitations of urban citizenship.

One of the limitations of urban citizenship is the focus on cities over rural areas; that is, it rests on what Bart Van Leeuwen (2010) describes as a "certain level of indifference" among residents of a larger urban area that allows "the possibility of personal freedom and a tolerant multicultural city" (639). However, as Jamie Winders (2012) reminds us:

> Immigrants are moving directly to American suburbs, bypassing the central city and destabilizing the spatial frameworks scholars and policymakers have used to evaluate neighborhood change, immigrant assimilation, race relations, and so on. Immigrants are also moving to new places, both skipping and leaving gateways such as Los Angeles in favor of locations in the U.S. South and elsewhere.
>
> (59)

This leads to Winders's concern about the different treatment undocumented migrants receive in different parts of the country and how different cities "see and do not see immigrants as local residents" (Winders 2012, 75). A more large-scale shift in reconceptualizing citizenship is necessary if all such community members are to be seen and heard.

Another issue is that even if a city is willing to issue municipal cards and serve as a sanctuary city, it cannot protect its community members from the federal government. For, as Rainer Bauböck (2003) notes, "[m]ost migrants' real destinations are cities rather than nation-states, but it is states that control migrants' movements and access to legal status" (707). Similarly, Els de Graauw (2012) warns:

> We cannot, however, discuss the emergence of urban citizenship in San Francisco without considering United States federalism and acknowledging San Francisco's continued subservience to the national government (as well as the state of California). The rights and benefits immigrants enjoy in San Francisco today are place-bound and therefore limited. City ID cards, for example, can only be used for intra-city affairs, and they do not confer legal status, give permission to drive, or increase cardholders' eligibility for public services.
>
> (147)

For these reasons, policy debates that occur on the state and federal level are of great import. Relatedly, it is necessary to identify and understand the conceptions of citizenship that underlie these larger debates. The very basic belief in who is—and who is not—a member of the community lead to much different positions on the protection and extension of rights of undocumented individuals. In moving away from the state, other realms become important; the geographic realm in terms of city and community, and the social realm as seen in contrast to—and connection with—the political sphere.

Social Citizenship

Several theorists have examined more socially constituted under-standings of citizenship; that is, the difference between being a citizen and acting as a citizen. Isin and Wood (1999) claim that citizenship "can be described as *both* a set of practices (cultural, symbolic and economic) and a bundle of rights and duties (civil, political and social) that define an individual's membership in a pol-ity" (4). They use this distinction between practice and status as a way of creating a balance between the particular (group identity) and the universal (nation-state identity). However, this reliance on group identity presumes a coherent, perhaps even insular, group—not differently situated (in terms of legal status) individuals within a geographic community.

Similar to Isin and Wood's argument, Kumar and Silver (1995) make a distinction between state and social citizenship. Or, as they put it:

> In our view, the value of citizenship in a liberal state has two dis-tinct facets. The first is that of standing in a certain relationship vis-à-vis the state. That standing entitles one to benefits just as it subjects one to duties that are and remain exclusively within the authority of the state to confer and in the purview of the state to demand. The second is that of standing, together with others, in a community of citizens united in a shared form of life.
>
> (71)

The authors use this distinction as a way of shedding light on the exclusion that occurs in their second understanding of citizenship, their example being "Don't Ask Don't Tell" policies in the United States military. I use this second understanding of citizenship, as standing together in a shared form of life, to reassess or augment the first understanding of a status derived in relation to the state.

Iris Marion Young also points to a more communal conception of citizenship. In addition to the traditional state-sanctioned notion of citizenship, she describes "two other senses of citizenship—having a common life with and being treated in the same way as the other citizens" (Young 1990, 115). These secondary meanings do not rely on political rights, but instead on a more social basis of shared experiences and communal obligations. The hope is that once social citizenship is recognized, equal treatment and consideration will be granted to *all* individuals that share the common life and fate of the community. Thus, focusing on the social sphere instead of the political sphere allows for greater recognition, and avenues to acknowledgement, of those individuals currently without standing in the political realm.

* * * * *

There is a range of other theories in which scholars have argued for new forms of citizenship that may help to navigate the current situation of migrant settlers. Harold Bauder, for example, argues for domicile citizenship. "A problem with contemporary state practices of citizenship," he writes, "is precisely that legal status rather than territorial presence tends to define migrants' access to citizenship. The domicile principle of citizenship, however, implies that citizenship is a right for everyone who is a de facto resident in a political territory, independent of status" (Bauder 2014, 97). Thus, one's physical presence is the only requirement of citizenship.

Other theorists point to different characteristics or actions that should warrant citizenship. For example, stakeholder citizenship claims that citizenship should be granted to those who have a stake in the future of the community. In all of these theories, there is a call to question and justify our criteria for citizenship, as well as an attempt to visualize what the nation-state would look like if such conceptions were put into practice. While many theorists question the metric currently being used to determine citizenship, there is limited agreement as to what that metric should be. My theory calls for a broader conception of citizenship based—not on location—but on the performance of citizen-like activities. In this formulation, the new metric would be acting out civic duties—paying taxes, contributing to the community, sharing in a common life. In other words, performing citizenship.

Performing Citizenship

Judith Butler (1990) famously and forcefully introduced the idea of performativity as a way of questioning essentialized notions of gender; that is, the idea that is there is an essence—a universal notion or Platonic form—of woman. She extends Simone de Beauvoir's (1949) argument that one is not born, but becomes, a woman. As opposed to biological sex, gender is not innate; it is a historically and socially constructed category. Butler uses the notion of performance as a way of questioning what is natural and what is socially constructed, as well as attempting to undermine the binary category of male/female.

While a different history and set of legal challenges, I use this idea of performativity to create a new understanding of citizenship and question the legal/illegal binary. If someone is acting like a citizen—performing those duties we claim citizens are obligated to do—should they not be seen as more than the legal construct of "unauthorized"? This, however, reveals a major difference between performing gender and performing citizenship: gender binaries are called into question by performances that do not enact accepted gendered behaviors and dress. In contrast, performing citizenship relies on the idea that the performance is the same; what differs, and what can potentially undermine existing categories, is that the unseen difference between similar performers (i.e., legal status) leads to very different circumstances.

In order to have an impact performing gender, the performance needs to be public and recurrent. Similarly, performing citizenship—to be recognized—must be repeated and requires a public component. One cannot show up, perform one act, and be granted citizenship (although that would be enough for domicile citizenship). In performance-based citizenship, one needs to be part of the community and actively engaged in the duties of citizenship. But, once an individual is performing her duties of citizenship, she should be recognized for fulfilling her political obligations. This recognition, in turn, should trigger certain state-granted protections and privileges.

*   *   *   *   *

In this chapter, I have attempted to highlight the positive and negative aspects of various theories of citizenship. It is important to note the range of scholars grappling with this issue of migration and the limits of nation-state granted status. I similarly claim that a reconceptualization of citizenship is necessary and that we must come up with a new metric to determine who should be recognized as members of our political community. As detailed in the following chapter, though, I argue that it can be better approached through a new understanding of political obligation, which, in turn, can serve as a stepping-stone toward the realization of performance-based citizenship. Thus, in the next chapter, I argue for rethinking political obligation as a first step toward extending citizenship to those undocumented individuals settled within our borders.

Notes

1 Joseph Carens (1995) extends Rawls's veil of ignorance to issues of immigration. He acknowledges that Rawls is theorizing about a closed community, but argues "that Rawls's approach is applicable to a broader context than the one he considers" (Carens 233). I agree that extending the device of the veil to global questions would alter the way we viewed certain issues of global justice, including immigration. However, I believe we have to look to other theorists or extend Rawls in a way he did not intend, as Rawls not only counters this attempt in his *Theory of Justice*, but does so more explicitly in *The Law of Peoples* (Rawls 1999, 8–9, 39). In addition, Rawls's work is used by other theorists to argue for a special and limited obligation we have to fellow citizens alone.

2 David Ingram (2003) describes this exclusion as

> unforgivable in light of the realities of our post-Westphalian world. Rawlsian political liberalism postulates the existence of closed, homogeneous nations in a way that explicitly brackets multicultural migration and diversity. To the extent that it acknowledges group rights at all, it is only within the context of illiberal undemocratic societies.
>
> (361)

3 This is a potentially problematic claim for contract theory and the role of consent as, in this scenario, an individual who actively chooses the society is seen as less of a member of the polity than is someone who tacitly consents by nature of her birth into a society. This will be treated in greater detail in the next chapter.

References

Amstutz, Mark R. 2013. *International Ethics: Concepts, Theories, and Cases in Global Politics*, 4th edition. Lanham: Rowman & Littlefield Publishers, Inc.

Bauböck, Rainer. 2003. "Towards a Political Theory of Migrant Nationalism." *International Migration Review*, Vol. 37, No. 3. Transnational Migration: International Perspectives (Fall), 700–723.

Bauder, Harald. 2014. "Domicile Citizenship, Human Mobility and Territoriality." *Progress in Human Geography*, Vol. 38, No. 1 (February), 91–106.

Beiner, Ronald. 1995. "Why Citizenship Constitutes a Theoretical Problem in the Last Decade of the Twentieth Century." In *Theorizing Citizenship*, edited by Ronald Beiner, 1–28. Albany: State University of New York Press.

Benhabib, Seyla. 2006. *Another Cosmopolitanism*. New York: Oxford University Press.

——.1996. "Toward a Deliberative Model of Democratic Legitimacy." In *Democracy and Difference: Contesting the Boundaries of the Political*. Princeton: Princeton University Press.

Butler, Judith. 1990. *Gender Trouble*. New York: Routledge.

Carens, Joseph H. 1995. "Aliens and Citizens: The Case for Open Borders." In *Theorizing Citizenship*, edited by Ronald Beiner, 229–253. Albany: State University of New York Press.

de Beauvoir, Simone. 2011 [1949]. *The Second Sex*. New York: Vintage Books.

de Graauw, Els. 2012. "The Inclusive City: Public-Private Partnerships and Immigrant Rights in San Francisco." In *Remaking Urban Citizenship: Organizations, Institutions, and the Right to the City*, Comparative Urban and Community Research, Volume 10, edited by Michael Peter Smith and Michael McQuarrie, 135–150. New Brunswick: Transaction Publishers.

Etzioni, Amitai. 1996a. *The New Golden Rule: Community and Morality in a Democratic Society*. New York: Basic Books.

——. 1996b. "A Moderate Communitarian Proposal." *Political Theory*, Vol. 24, No. 2 (May), 155–171.

Gaige, Mark P. 2008. "Citizen: Past Practices, Prospective Patterns." In *The Future of Citizenship*, edited by J. V. Ciprut, 121–143. Cambridge: MIT Press.

Glendon, Mary Ann. 1991. *Rights Talk: The Impoverishment of Political Discourse*. New York: The Free Press.

Heater, Derek. 2002. *World Citizenship: Cosmopolitan Thinking and Its Opponents*. New York: Continuum Studies in Citizenship.

Hollinger, David A. 1998. "Nationalism, Cosmopolitanism, and the United States." In *Immigration and Citizenship in the Twenty-First Century*, edited by Noah M. J. Pickus, 85–99. Lanham: Rowman & Littlefield Publishers, Inc.

Honig, Bonnie. 1997a. *Democracy and the Foreigner*. Princeton: Princeton University Press.

——. 1997b. "Ruth, The Model Emigrée: Mourning and the Symbolic Politics of Immigration." *Political Theory*, Vol. 25, No. 1 (February), 112–136.

Ingram, David. 2003. "Between Political Liberalism and Postnational Cosmopolitanism: Toward an Alternative Theory of Human Rights." *Political Theory*, Vol. 31, No. 3 (June), 359–391.

Isin, Engin F. and Patricia K. Wood. 1999. *Citizenship and Identity*. London: Sage Publications, Ltd.

Kingsbury, Damien. 2007. *Political Development*. New York: Routledge.

Kumar, Rahul and David Silver. 1995. "The Ethics of Exclusion." In *Theorizing Citizenship*, edited by Ronald Beiner. Albany: State University of New York Press.

Kymlicka, Will. 1995. *Multicultural Citizenship: A Liberal Theory of Minority Rights*. Oxford: Clarendon Press.

———. 1989. *Liberalism, Community and Culture*. Oxford: Clarendon Press.

MacIntyre, Alasdair, Donald P. Kommers and W. David Solomon. 1990. "The Privatization of Good: An Inaugural Lecture." *The Review of Politics*, Vol. 52, No. 3 (Summer), 344–377.

Mills, Charles W. 1999. *The Racial Contract*. Ithaca, NY: Cornell University Press.

Nyers, Peter. 2010. "No One is Illegal between City and Nation." *Studies in Social Justice*, Vol. 4, No. 2 (June), 127–143.

Okin, Susan Moller. 1987. "Justice and Gender." *Philosophy and Public Affairs*, Vol. 16, No. 1 (Winter), 42–72.

Oldfield, Adrian. 1990. *Citizenship and Community, Civic Republicanism and the Modern World*. London: Routledge.

Parekh, Bhiku. 2003. "Cosmopolitanism and Global Citizenship." *Review of International Studies*, Vol. 29, No. 1 (January), 3–17.

Pateman, Carole. 1988. *The Sexual Contract*. Stanford: Stanford University Press.

Pateman, Carole and Charles Mills. 2007. *Contract and Domination*. Cambridge: Polity Press.

Rawls, John. 2001. *Justice as Fairness: A Restatement*. Cambridge: Harvard University Press.

———. 1999. *The Law of Peoples*. Cambridge: Harvard University Press.

———. 1985. "Justice as Fairness: Political Not Metaphysical." *Philosophy and Public Affairs*, Vol. 14, No. 3 (Summer), 223–251.

———. 1971. *A Theory of Justice*. Cambridge: Harvard University Press.

Roshan Samar, Tony. 2012. "Citizens in Search of a City: Towards a New Infrastructure of Political Belonging." In *Remaking Urban Citizenship: Organizations, Institutions, and the Right to the City*, Compartive Urban and Community Research, Volume 10, edited by Michael Peter Smith & Michael McQuarrie, 39–56. New Brunswick: Transaction Publishers.

Sandel, Michael. 1996. *Democracy's Discontent: America in Search of a Public Philosophy*. Cambridge: Harvard University Press.

———. 1984. "The Procedural Republic and the Unencumbered Self." *Political Theory*, Vol. 12, No. 1 (February), 81–96.

———. 1982. *Liberalism and the Limits of Justice*. Cambridge: Cambridge University Press.

Taylor, Charles. 1994. "The Politics of Recognition." In *Multiculturalism: Examining the Politics of Recognition*, edited by Amy Gutmann, 25–74. Princeton: Princeton University Press.

Van Leeuwen, Bart. 2010. "Dealing with Urban Diversity: Promises and Challenges of City Life for Intercultural Citizenship." *Political Theory,* Vol. 38, No. 5 (October), 631–657.

Walzer, Michael. 1990. "The Communitarian Critique of Liberalism." *Political Theory*, Vol. 18, No. 1 (February), 6–23.

Winders, Jamie. 2012. "Seeing Immigrants: Institutional Visibility and Immigrant Incorporation in New Immigrant Destinations." *ANNALS, AAPSS*, Vol. 641, No. 1 (May), 58–77.

Young, Iris Marion. 1990. "Polity and Group Difference: A Critique of the Ideal of Universal Citizenship." In *Throwing Like a Girl and Other Essays in Feminist Philosophy and Social Theory*, 114–137. Bloomington: Indiana University Press.

3 Flipping Our Understandings of Political Obligation

This is about citizenship. And how do you define citizenship? Do you look to the bureaucrats in Washington, D.C., the Department of Immigration and Naturalization Services, and let them define what it means to be a citizen? . . . These are great citizens. These are people that are working hard. They're doing the work that many people can't do or won't do. They help us immensely in our economy. They're trying to better themselves. They're trying to go to college. These are the—the characteristics and the traits of good citizens. That, in and of itself, has earned them the right—my goodness, at the very least—to be able to pay an in-state tuition rate.

—Senator Cronin (Republican)[1]

In defending Illinois's version of the DREAM Act, Senator Cronin argues for the extension of a benefit to undocumented residents by questioning our conception of citizenship. His understanding of "great citizens" does not rely on nation-state status but on the actions and characteristics of the individual. While he concludes that such traits should at least warrant in-state tuition, I argue that performing citizenship in the way he describes—working, contributing to the economy, bettering themselves and their community—should trigger a host of protections and privileges usually reserved for citizens. Senator Cronin's "citizens," unauthorized by the nation-state, highlight the disconnection between paper citizenship and performing citizenship, and expose the gap between the reality of our neighborhoods and conventional theories of citizenship and political obligation.

While many theorists—as discussed in the previous chapter—argue that we should change our conceptions of citizenship, my central claim is that we can best accomplish this goal by altering our understanding of political obligation. The political obligation literature typically asks what we, as citizens, owe our state. In contrast, I flip that understanding of political obligation and ask what the state owes to those who perform the role of citizen, regardless of their documented status. The existing literature also provides a basis for arguing that performing citizenship is inextricably linked to protections and goods provided by the state. As such, the very premise of United States political philosophy—contract theory and political obligation—can be used to fundamentally alter the way we determine citizenship.

My argument also has implications for claims about the role of voluntary consent as a legitimizing step in submitting to state authority. By moving here and continuing to work and live in the United States, migrants have actively consented to the authority of the state in a way that most native-born citizens have not. Yet, the undocumented do not have a voice in the laws to which they submit. This situation highlights the disjunction between consent and autonomy in conceptions of political obligation. To be sure, my account is not the only one to raise issue with theories of political obligation. As discussed in greater detail below, previous scholarship has identified a number of problems with the concept of political obligation. Before turning to these critiques, however, it is necessary to provide a brief overview of conventional theories of political obligation.

Theories of Political Obligation

T.H. Green's stated purpose, in his foundational text on political obligation, is "to discover the true ground or justification for obedience to law" (Green, 13). Since that time, political obligation has been understood, in its most basic form, as an individual's moral requirement to obey the law and support the state by fulfilling certain duties. Recent theorists have attempted to extend both the understanding of political obligation and its underlying justifications. John Horton (2010), for example, claims that

> [p]olitical obligation is not necessarily reducible simply to an obligation to obey the law of the polity of which one is a member. There may be other obligations or responsibilities specifically deriving from one's membership of a particular polity, such as a duty to vote, to serve one's country in times of crisis or even to oppose injustice perpetrated by one's own government,

which are not enshrined in the law and, which if not observed, do not incur a legal penalty.

(14)

Thus, the range of obligations understood to be owed to one's state has expanded, and has done so in ways that are increasingly hard to articulate. That is, accounts of citizen's duties to the polity have moved beyond clearly defined activities—such as following the law and voting—into other more amorphous ways in which we engage in a common life. I build on this point further in this chapter when determining what duties are necessary to trigger performance-based citizenship.

The most common justification for shouldering these duties—at least historically—has been that political obligation is born of consent. Obligation, therefore, is a result of contract theory. In its most basic form, contract theory tells a tale of individuals coming together to create society. People leave the ungoverned state of nature to create a sovereign authority that has a common power over them with the ability to judge, punish, and protect individuals and their rights. To this end, these enlightened inhabitants of the state of nature enter into a social compact in which they agree to abide by common laws with the understanding that the power of the laws derives from each individual. Thus, the resulting idea is that—if political authority is legitimate—we are all authors of the laws to which we submit. In consenting to the contract, the members agree—not only to obey the authority of the state—but to honor obligations to the state and to their fellow citizens. The founding myth of the Unites States, for example, is often told in the form of this original moment in social contract theory.

There have been many criticisms of social contract theory and the role of consent in creating political obligations. The most common question is why those not present when the contract was signed are still bound by it and its ensuing obligations. Locke foresaw these concerns and provided an account of tacit consent.

> The difficulty is, what ought to be looked upon as a *tacit consent*, and how far it binds, i.e. how far any one shall be looked on to have consented, and thereby submitted to any government, where he has made no expressions of it at all. And to this I say, that every man, that hath any possessions, or enjoyment, of any part of the dominions of any government, doth thereby give his *tacit consent*, and is as far forth obliged to obedience

> to the laws of that government, during such enjoyment, as any one under it; whether this his possession be of land, to him and his heirs for ever, or a lodging only for a week; or whether it be barely travelling freely on the highway.
>
> (Locke 1980 [1690], 64)

Therefore, even those residents who did not explicitly agree to the contract have tacitly consented to the legitimacy of the state by remaining in the state and benefitting from certain public goods. However, those giving tacit consent are viewed by Locke as less committed members of society than those who explicitly stated their intent to be a member of the political community. This can be seen in the ease of exit as Locke provides that

> whenever the owner, who has given nothing but such a tacit consent to the government, will by donation, sale, or otherwise quit the said possession, he is at liberty to go and incorporate himself into any other commonwealth, or to agree with others to begin a new one, in vacuis locis, in any part of the world they can find free and unpossessed.
>
> (Locke 1980 [1690], 64–65)

The obverse of this exit option is that, as long as you stay and keep your possessions, you are granting tacit consent to the sovereign power.

Given the lack of "free and unpossessed" land in modern times, those claiming the existence of tacit consent must rely on more than failure to leave the state. One such argument points to the lack of open rebellion as evidence of tacit consent with the idea that, if we are not explicitly questioning state authority, we are tacitly accepting it. Another justification for political legitimacy not requiring explicit consent looks to the merit of state policies. Steven DeLue (1989), for example, argues that

> even if the state affords citizens no basis upon which to give their formal and direct acceptance of the state, still, as long as the state supports policies citizens accept, then citizens live in a society they *could* give their consent to, if given a formal way to do so.
>
> (131)

In this formulation, legitimacy appears to be retroactively granted when the state uses its power to create acceptable policies, relegating popular sovereignty to a more evaluative function.

There has also been an attempt to bolster the notion of tacit consent with the discussion of "consent-implying" acts. These acts can include voting or jury duty—which provide the most clear-cut cases of supporting the larger political and juridical structure—but also less intentioned acts such as driving on public highways. The latter reflects the benefits public works provide each individual and mirrors Locke's inclusion of the enjoyment of any part of the dominions of government. The former speaks to a much more purposeful performance and parallels duties of political obligation. But what about those individuals barred from voting or serving as jurors? There must be other activities that also reflect a high level of engagement required by performing citizenship in which the individual is rooted in her place of residence, identifies with her community, and contributes to the larger cooperative scheme necessary for a sustained shared life.

In recent years, several scholars have revisited and expanded theories of political obligation in an attempt to defend it against its critics and to breathe new life into the concept. George Klosko, one of the foremost proponents of political obligation, acknowledges in a 2004 article that "[a]t the present time, it is widely believed that there is no satisfactory theory of political obligation" before attempting to provide one (Klosko 2004, 801). One of the ways Klosko and other recent theorists have extended arguments for political obligation is by adding potential justifications for incurring political obligations. One such justification incorporates consent-implying acts and points to the benefits individuals derive from public works. These public works go beyond infrastructure to include social services. The idea is that the state is the only mechanism for ensuring certain public benefits and that the bestowal of said benefits earn the gratitude of the citizenry which, in turn, results in their willingness to perform certain duties (e.g., see Klosko 2008). The gratitude theory of political obligation has been used to explain not only citizens' obligation to the state but the creation of special relationships and duties among citizens. Klosko (2009) describes these compatriot preferences as necessary to provide public goods on which we all rely, some of us more than others (243–265). This theory blends a pragmatic approach with a potentially idealized vision of human appreciation—or even awareness—of the goods provided by government and taxes paid by fellow compatriots.

An idealized vision of human sentiment is also reflected in the fairness justification for political obligation. The basic premise here is that it is unfair for an individual to benefit from a scheme if she does not share in the various responsibilities or sacrifices necessary to ensure the success of said cooperative scheme. In addition, the scheme itself must be fair in terms of the distribution of resources. Horton (2010) describes the justification for this theory as follows:

> It is insufficient, according to fair-play theory, that a scheme of social cooperation be mutually beneficial: if it is to generate the appropriate obligation, it must also be fair. The reason for this is that people should not be expected to accept that they are under an obligation to support a cooperative scheme, including those from which they benefit, if the distribution of the benefits and burdens arising from it is unfair.
>
> (91)

One concern that has been raised in relation to fairness or fair-play theory is that it may lead to less buy-in on goods that do not benefit everyone (e.g., see Klosko 2004). That is, it is one thing to justify fair outcomes for mutually beneficial programs; it is quite another to agree to sacrifice for programs that will always only benefit a set group of people, even if that set group is the least advantaged of society. Yet, certain social services—such as means-tested programs—are exactly the kind of public good that require the coordination of the state and the sacrifice of a majority of citizens. For our purposes, fair-play theory can be used to highlight the issue of undocumented residents contributing to social security and paying taxes while getting nothing in return. This asymmetry is not mutually beneficial and speaks to the inequity of the current distribution of resources. In order to rectify this, and to honor the special relationship among those taking part in the cooperative scheme, undocumented residents would need to be included in the fair distribution of public goods.

In arguing for the existence of political obligation, Margaret Gilbert provides an associative form of membership that is beyond the typical conceptions of citizenship. Her plural subject theory of political obligation provides that

> the members of a political society are obligated to uphold its political institutions by virtue of their membership in that society. That membership is a matter of participation in a joint commitment to accept together with the other members the political institutions in question.
>
> (Gilbert 2008, 289)

This idea of membership in a society premised on participation in a joint venture provides an informative glimpse of a political community predicated—not on documents—but on the actions of the individual. That is, if obligation is born of a shared social commitment, can sharing in that joint venture trigger state-conferred rights and protections? I explore and extend this idea below, but first I will turn to some of the more noted criticisms of political obligation.

Problems of Political Obligation

In the conventional formulation of political obligation, the focus is on the individual's obligation to the state or community, not on the state or community's obligation to the individual. This is the core issue that I aim to redress. However, there are other important critiques that should be noted as they have helped to deepen our understanding and shape future iterations of conceptions of political obligation.

Bhikhu Parekh observes the continued limitation of understandings of political obligation. He claims "[t]here is hardly a political theorist writing on the subject today who does not think that political obligation is about obeying the civil authority (Parekh 1993, 237)." Related to this formulation of political obligation as obedience is the idea that our obligation is derived from the action of consenting to the state, thereby legitimating state authority over its residents. Patrick Riley (1992) explains "[t]he modern contractarian position involves an effort to view politics as legitimized through consent, through special volition, so that obligation and authority are products of everyone's original freedom and responsibility, effects of everyone's will as a moral cause" (8). Several theorists, notably Carole Pateman and A. John Simmons, have noted the resulting paradox: we are involuntarily bound to the authority of the state because we supposedly voluntarily consented to that authority.

In *The Problem of Political Obligation*, Pateman (1985) writes that "[c]onsent theory has long been embarrassed by the fact that it always runs into difficulties when confronted by the demand to show who has, and when, and how, actually and explicitly consented in the liberal democratic state" (15). This is further problematized by the argument "that even if citizens cannot, with any plausibility, be said to have promised or consented, they are, nevertheless, politically obligated in the liberal democratic state" (Pateman 1985, 3). This paradox has led philosophical anarchists to claim that, if we follow the logic of consent, no government is legitimate

44 *Flipping Our Understandings*

(e.g., see Wolff 1998). The premise of their argument is that humans are morally obligated to be autonomous; submitting only to those laws that they themselves author. The only legitimate state authority, by their account, is one in which this connection is not severed. Such a conception of self-governance is in clear contradiction with the idea that we must obey all laws and honor the legitimacy of the state regardless of the tenuous nature of our representation.

Pateman notes the horizontal nature of political obligation in that it is perceived as not only a relationship with the state, but a relationship among citizens. She sees this as incompatible with the more horizontal "liberal conception of the 'political'" and calls for "a revised democratic conception," described as follows:

> The members of the community are citizens in many political associations, which are bound together through horizontal and multifaceted ties of self-assumed political obligation. The essential feature of a democratic revision of the "political" is that it is no longer conceived as separate from everyday life. The political sphere is one dimension, the collective dimension, of social life as a whole. It is the area of social existence in which citizens voluntarily cooperate together and sustain their common life and common undertaking.
>
> (Pateman 1985, 174)

It is this idea of a socially derived collective enterprise that has been relied on by more recent iterations of political obligation. Gilbert's above-mentioned plural subject theory, for example, makes use of this concept. So, too, does Horton's associative model, which describes political obligation resulting not from consent—tacit or otherwise—but created through associative duties arising from social practices (Horton 2010).

The idea that political ties come about through the cooperative undertaking of sustaining a common life has powerful implications. So much so, in fact, that the concept can be used to broaden our understanding of citizenship and, consequently, expand the community to whom we owe certain obligations. That is, who is included in this cooperative undertaking? Who is contributing to our common life through labor, military service, tax dollars, and volunteer work? If someone is repeatedly engaged in building the community and contributing to a shared life, should they not be considered as members of our community deserving of legal protections and a portion of the produce of our cooperative scheme? Thus, those individuals performing citizenship can be seen as members of this mutually obligated community regardless of nation-state authorization.

Simmons's critique of political obligation also provides important building blocks for broadening our understanding of citizenship and political obligation. He begins his detailed examination of the topic in *Moral Principles and Political Obligation* by setting out the "three central areas of disagreement" about political obligation: "To whom is this obligation owed? What is this obligation an obligation to do? How does one come to be under this obligation?" (Simmons 1979, 3). Simmons ultimately concludes that "political theory cannot offer a convincing general account of our political bonds" (Simmons 1979, 192). My account, however, uses these same important questions to draw a much different conclusion. I argue, instead, that the state is bound to do more than it is currently doing in regards to undocumented individuals living within its borders. Indeed, the three areas adroitly identified by Simmons—the how, the who, and the what of political obligation—provide the greatest leverage into altering understandings of the relationships and duties created by consent-implying acts. In turn, this new way of conceptualizing political obligation establishes a basis for the recognition and legal protection of those performing citizenship. In the next section, I take each of these three areas in turn and provide alternative ways of thinking about what is owed to whom and why.

Reconceptualizing Political Obligation

The core of my argument is that we should flip our understandings of political obligation. Instead of the traditional argument that we are obliged to perform certain civic duties as a result of the benefits and protections supplied by the state, those same duties—repeatedly performing citizenship—should trigger access to public goods and legal protections. The criteria to attain citizenship rights, then, and the metric to determine who is a member of the political community are based on an individual's sustained performance as a citizen.

This switch in focus—from obligations owed by the individual to those owed by the state—also alters other aspects of political obligation. It changes the way we think about what is owed, why it is owed, and to whom we owe special obligations. Yet, as I argue below, the definitions of duties and the descriptions of community provided by conventional accounts of political obligation can similarly be used in my reconceptualization. The result, however, leads to far different ideas of inclusion and a fundamentally altered vision of the polis.

To Whom Do We Owe Special Obligations?

Political obligation is not just owed to the state; it also includes special obligations to fellow compatriots. Thus, the relationship is not only between the individual and the state, but also among members of the polity. This relationship is predicated on belonging to the same political community and results in special obligations we owe our fellow nationals that we do not owe to individuals outside of the state. This is why patriotism is often pitted against cosmopolitanism with the argument that—far from being citizens of the world with global obligations—there are moral, rational, and defensible reasons to privilege the needs of fellow citizens above international concerns. The underlying issues are determining who constitutes the people (that is, who is the "us" and who is the "them") and ascertaining any resulting obligations that arise from the special relationship among those included in the "us." If we grant that we do owe special obligations to fellow citizens—obligations that surpass those owed to those outside the political community—what is the metric we use to determine who *are* our fellow "citizens"? Is it limited to those authorized by the nation-state—bearing the stamp of state-granted citizenship—or is there something more we mean when we evoke the concept of citizen? If, by citizen, we mean a fellow member of a cooperative undertaking to sustain our common life, then the "us" is larger than currently considered.

One of the issues Simmons raises regarding theories of political obligation is the assumption of particularism, that an individual would be bound "to one particular state above all others, namely that state in which he is a citizen" (Simmons 1981, 31–32). Yet, Simmons claims that proximity is not sufficient to trigger this particular moral obligation. "Most of us do not, of course, regard mere residence as significant in this way," he writes, "for we do not believe the political obligations of citizens to be identical to the obligations of visiting aliens" (Simmons 1981, 34). But why not? What is different about that relationship? What triggers this particular moral obligation? Intention matters here. Is the "visiting alien" residing in the nation for a set amount of time with no intention of sharing in the fate of the community or does she aspire to rootedness within the community? If the latter, why would two seemingly similar people—living the same amount of years in the same place, paying taxes, contributing to a shared life—not have identical obligations? And, more importantly for my purposes, why would these two similarly situated people not have identical protections? A morally defensible answer must be based on more than a federal document.

Altering the criteria for inclusion in the political community also changes the body of people with access to the political process and lawmakers. Within theoretical notions of popular sovereignty, there would be many more authors of the laws and, as some would argue, would include those who broke immigration laws in order to now be in that group. It is a common belief that continuing to live in violation of federal immigration laws should necessarily bar that person from ever being part of the political community. Such continued law breaking may also be problematic for a theory based on political obligation, given its traditional focus on justifications for obeying the law. However, being present within the nation without documents is a civil, not criminal, offense comparable to littering or driving over the speed limit. If we were to ban speedy drivers from the political community, many of us would be excluded. Immigration laws and speeding laws are quite different, especially in terms of political rights. However, a civil offense does not seem sufficient to bar a person from being considered for citizenship. The history of shifting immigration regimes, as discussed in Chapter One, also provides potential reasons to not accept the violation of immigration laws as an automatic reason to be excluded.

Democratic legitimacy requires a set membership; that is, a group of people known, publicly acknowledged, and accountable to each other. It is one thing to follow the laws of a nation as a tourist, quite another to be part of the political body that legitimates those laws. Stephen Macedo (2007) claims that "[b]orders are morally significant because they bound systems of collective self-governance" (73). This speaks to the need to have a bounded and accountable political membership. However, this claim raises new questions. Does the moral significance of the border refer to nationality, residence, or some other designation of belonging? And what metric is used to determine who is included in that political membership: documents or the carrying out of duties and obligations?

In thinking through these questions, the work of theorists writing about political obligation or the special duties of citizenship are, once again, informative. For example, Parekh (2003) provides the following explanation as to why we owe special obligations to our fellow citizens:

> They see their community as theirs, feel a particular sense of responsibility for it, experience pride and shame when it

does or does not live up to certain ideals, and take interest in its problems. The sense of gratitude for the benefits received, the principle of fair play, enlightened self-interest and a feeling of identification with the community give rise to a wide range of obligations to their community and fellow-citizens. The latter have a special claim on them, and it is stronger than that of the outsiders. No common life can be built and sustained if the members of a community felt no special sense of responsibility for each other and treated each other as they would outsiders.

(8–9)

Parekh sketches a vision of a community of people with a sense of shared fate who contribute to society. Their insider status is not derived per se from citizenship granted by the nation-state. The depth and richness of the connections he describes, in fact, have everything to do with a common social life, not legal status. It is the actions and sentiments that bond the community and lead to a special sense of responsibility. They are acting in ways that identify them as community members. They are performing citizenship.

Similarly, in defending special relationships among citizens, Klosko (2009) explains that "the compatriot preferences that interest us are owed to fellow citizens, not *qua* fellow citizens but as fellow participants in cooperative schemes that provide public goods without which we could not lead acceptable lives" (254). Those living and working in our communities, engaged in the civic life of our cities, and sharing a common life would fit the bill—regardless of nation-state-granted status. Klosko proceeds to provide a rule for equal participation in which

all individuals required to contribute should have equal say in deciding what the standard of fair distribution should be and, reflexively, the nature of the decision procedures themselves, through which such decisions should be made. In order for people's political obligations to be morally defensible, they must have rights to participate in decisions about the standards of justice the relevant institutions embody.

(Klosko 2009, 258)

His claim for access—and in fact his threat to the moral defensibility of political obligation—rests on determining which individuals are required to contribute. This, once again, raises the question of what actions count in determining inclusion and how one becomes obligated to the state and polity.

How Does One Become Obligated?

As discussed above, there has been an attempt to use "consent-implying" acts as the vehicle for legitimating state authority and justifying the binding nature of political obligation. These acts are exactly the type of activities that undocumented residents do. They work, pay taxes, serve in the military, volunteer in their communities, and generally contribute to the cooperative undertaking of sustaining a common life. Yet, they are not considered part of the larger nation or party to the longstanding social contract. Furthermore, migrants are in the minority of people that have taken a proactive action to choose this state instead of merely being born into it, the explicit consent of Locke's engaged citizens. Instead of seeing this as proof of their desire to be an active member of the polity, it is seen as a reason to exclude them from certain benefits and privileges.

Even theorists that defend minority and group rights put voluntary migrants in their own category (e.g., see Gutmann 1993, and Kymlicka 1995). This is largely an issue of what is seen as a voluntary choice on the part of the migrant and the potentially unfair demands placed on the receiving state. Why should the receiving state be obligated to ensure the health, well-being, and cultural survival of individuals who were neither invited nor authorized by the state? To some, the act of migration signals a choice to give up citizenship rights granted by the sending community—a version of Locke's exit clause. However, as a noncitizen and unauthorized resident, the migrant has no right to make claims against the receiving community. In this situation, the active choice to live in the United States is not seen as a necessary step in legitimating political authority. Rather, it is viewed as consent to be punished by a system of which one cannot be a part; a system that has the power to detain and deport the very individual that actively chose to be a member of the polity.

These theoretical conclusions are largely a result of excluding the unauthorized individual from the strains of reciprocity. The unauthorized immigrant is an outsider in both liberal theory and liberal democratic practice. Instead, those engaged in consent-implying acts should be seen as a partner in the special relationship with the state and larger polity. By flipping our understanding of political obligation and focusing on the performance of duties, the Achilles heel of political obligation theory—the voluntarist nature of consent—becomes the basis for the expansion of rights. Instead of being used as a justification for state power and civilian obedience, carrying out consent-implying acts—especially those sustained and repeated actions that contribute to the cooperative scheme of society—should obligate the state to protect those performing citizenship. Thus, the "one" who becomes obligated is the state. That is, instead of the individual becoming obligated to perform certain duties for the state, it is the state that becomes obligated to the individual when the individual performs certain civic duties. So, if performing citizenship has created an obligation on the part of the state, what is that obligation?

What Is This an Obligation to Do?

Within traditional constructions of political obligation, once the *who* and the *how* have been answered, the argument shifts to *what* a citizen is obligated to do. But now that the onus is on the state— the state now being the who—what does this mean in terms of what should be expected of the state? Again, conventional theories of political obligation are informative but insufficient. At the least, I would like to suggest that it is exactly the actions of the state that supposedly bind us to our obligations that are now required to be provided for those performing citizenship.

Returning then to the aforementioned gratitude theory of political obligation, in which citizens carry out their civic duties out of gratitude for the state, the state provides for the common good. Part of why the state engenders special obligations is due to the fact that the state can provide certain public goods that other systems or structures either cannot or will not. Such goods include national defense, a system of justice, and social services. Thus, those performing citizenship should be granted protection through the justice system—from crime and exploitation as well as protection from the state—and be provided access to social services.

Folding in the fairness justification for political obligation, those who contribute to the common good have a claim to fair distribution of those goods as well as a voice in determining distribution. Undocumented individuals living within our communities pay taxes, join the military, and contribute to the gross domestic product (GDP). These contributions are directly linked to the common good, general defense, and public services. Thus, to carry through with the promise of the fairness theory, in addition to the protections and social services listed above, those performing citizenship should also have access to the political process. In extending the right to vote, the circle is complete. The performance can now include the most fundamental political obligation of all: voting, and with it voice, recognition, and standing within the political community.

What Performances Count?

If we are to accept a broader vision of citizenship, in which performing citizen-like duties triggers state protections and warrants some level of recognition and reciprocity, we need to identify what duties count. That is, if we are to move backwards from duties and obligations to rights and protections, we must identify those who are performing their community-based civic duties in order to extend to them performance-based citizenship. Is it enough to pay taxes? Must you be an active member in the civil society of your community? The underlying question is what we expect from each other as members of a bounded community who are jointly responsible for legitimating the authority of the laws. However, the enumeration of activities, characteristics, and expectations—that is, what the performance of citizenship looks like—is particularly difficult to articulate.

T. H. Marshall acknowledged that citizen duties are not as obvious or precise as citizen rights. While paying taxes and military service are clear duties, he added that other duties "are included in the general obligation to live the life of a good citizen, giving such service as one can to promote the welfare of the community" (Marshall 1950, 78). Similarly, Horton (2010) provides the following account:

> Moreover, there is more to political life than law, regulation and government, fundamental though those are. Thus, one can manifest one's political obligations by supporting one's polity in other ways, such as voting (even when this is not a legal obligation), participating in political affairs and generally being a good citizen, whatever that amounts to in any particular polity.
> (191)

Such vague general obligations are hard to quantify. After all, what does it mean to be a good citizen in a particular polity? In addition, we need a consistent metric of what we value in good citizens so we do not include only those characteristics society can use or exploit. Discussions surrounding the Development, Relief, and Education for Alien Minors (DREAM) Act speak to these concerns, as well as parallel some of my larger arguments.

Proponents of the DREAM Act justify granting conditional permanent residency (starting the path to citizenship) to those individuals who agree to attend college or join the military. The argument is threefold. First, the United States will benefit by granting status to those who either will be productive members of society (at least educated ones) or are willing to do the very civic duty of fighting for the country. In both cases, the focus is on the actions of the individual; that is, what they will contribute to the state. Their contributions, in turn, trigger state recognition. Secondly, the individuals that would be eligible to benefit from the DREAM Act are those who have lived in the United States for at least five years. This echoes intuitions that a person who has lived here for a certain amount of time is already rooted in our community. The third portion of the argument is that the beneficiaries in question were brought to this country by their parents; thus removing blame for the act of entering and remaining within the United States without nation-state authorization.

There are two aspects of these justifications that I find problematic. First, that the actions required are above and beyond normal measures of civic engagement. This is especially true for those who join the military in order to qualify. We are asking them to be prepared to sacrifice their lives in order to start the process of recognition; quite a high cost indeed. Secondly, the need to see the individual as blameless—the innocent child brought to the United States through no fault of their own—leads to the incrimination of the parents who, assumedly, have also lived in the United States at least five years and have been performing citizen-like duties during that time. Assuming that the parents are indeed performing citizenship, their contribution to the community needs to be acknowledged as well.

In recent years, Joseph Carens has mitigated his original stance regarding open borders, acknowledging that the nation-state has some rights to restrict entry into the political community. However, Carens believes that at some point the state's claims are outweighed by a migrant's moral claim to have her social membership legally recognized (Carens 2009 and 2013). He acknowledges that what is really "at stake is a person's ability to maintain and develop a rich and highly particular set of human ties" (Carens 2013, 164). Nevertheless, he argues that time and residence are sufficient proxies for these deeper ties. Carens similarly writes that certain "circumstances—arriving as children or marrying citizens or permanent residents—may accelerate or strengthen their moral claims to stay, but the most important consideration is the passage of time" (Carens 2013, 147). He admits that any benchmark—that is, the amount of time—is arbitrary, but argues that residing in a country for five years seems like a defensible statute of limitations.

Similarly, Elizabeth Cohen (2015) discusses the use of time in the naturalization process, noting that the five-year residence requirement is "widely understood to represent something that is central to citizenliness" (339). She goes on to write, "[i]n liberal democratic states, time elegantly translates abstract traits like loyalty and civic virtue into tangible political rights while maintaining the kind of uniformity that is often equated with egalitarianism" (Cohen 2015, 340). Thus, we understand that time is merely a proxy for what we are really trying to measure; but how can we articulate and quantify "citizenliness"?

The focus on time lapsed has practical merit in that it is easily identifiable and provable in a way that being generally a good citizen is not. It also seems to have intuitive appeal, evidenced by the fact that amnesty policies include length of time as a criterion. For example, in order to qualify for amnesty under the Immigration and Reform Control Act (IRCA) of 1986, an individual had to prove they continuously resided in the United States since January 1, 1982. Likewise, the Deferred Action for Childhood Arrivals (DACA) program applies only to those who have lived continuously in the United States for at least five years. However, the focus on time masks the underlying justification for such a proposal. An individual might have a moral claim, not because she managed to elude detection for five years, but because she weaved herself into the fabric of her society and entered into the reciprocal relationship of mutual dependence among fellow citizens.

If time is not used as a proxy, how can we determine who is performing citizenship and who is not? As mentioned above, previous amnesty attempts have focused on time in residence. In addition, all acts have required that the individual not be a felon. That seems like a pretty low bar, although informative in terms of policies aimed at deporting only those individuals who have committed a felony. Barring criminal records and time in residence, what other characteristics or activities should be taken into account? Should there be some sort of calculus to determine when an individual reaches the level of performance that warrants the recognition of citizenship? Underlying this issue are several additional concerns. Are different activities weighted differently? How do we take gender and class differences into account when determining acceptable levels of performance? Can someone lose citizenship for the inability to perform actions? What if someone is performing citizenship for show, but does not have the emotional attachment and sense of shared fate it is meant to convey? I will discuss each of these in turn.

As seen above, the political obligation literature is suggestive, but vague, in terms of what activities count as duties of citizenship. The civic obligations that are clear and able to be proven are voting, jury duty, paying taxes, and joining the military. The first two obligations cannot be performed by undocumented individuals as they are banned from jury duty and federal voting, with very few local governments allowing noncitizens to vote. As a result, while voting in elections in which they are allowed to take part can be seen as part of the performance, the opportunities are too limited to include as an actual requirement. Paying taxes, however, can be included and is carried out by undocumented residents. Fighting for one's country is a clear political obligation and an activity that has been used to earn citizenship at different points in the history of the United States. Since 9/11, the United States has offered expedited citizenship as a way to aid recruitment efforts. As mentioned above, enlisting in the military is one of the avenues to receiving deferred action under the DACA program and is similarly included in the proposed federal DREAM Act. Yet, military service is asking an individual to potentially sacrifice her life. Such a perilous request cannot be one of the only ways to perform citizenship. What, then, are such activities? What counts as contributing to a common life?

At the risk of appearing to punt, I believe this is something that will be formed through discussions and deliberations as we begin to talk about what it means to be a citizen, who shares our fate, and what activities are viewed as contributing to a cooperative undertaking to sustain our common life. My argument, that the varied answers to these questions will include far more than nation-state authorization, is merely beginning a much larger conversation. That being said, I would like to suggest some candidates for inclusion as well as point to, in the next two chapters, activities and characteristics that state lawmakers believe signal inclusion into the political community. While paying taxes is a recurring theme, so is standing shoulder-to-shoulder with other state residents, be that while studying, working, or engaging in the life of the community. I would add such activities as taking part in the PTA, playing sports or watching community athletic events, attending parades and other civic festivals, babysitting for a neighbor, raising one's own children, sweeping one's driveway, and picking up the occasional piece of litter. This may all sound petty, but it is part of how we sustain a common life, imbricate ourselves within our communities, and develop a sense of shared fate with other members of the state. While you certainly may be inclined to pick up a piece of litter while traveling to other countries and communities, there is a different sense of duty and stewardship when it is in your own area of residence. It is this sense of ownership and belonging that leads to the loyalty desired by theorists of political obligation and citizenship.

Another concern is whether different activities should be weighted differently. That is, should there be some sort of calculus in which military service counts for twenty and picking up a piece of litter counts for half of one point. Tied to this concern as well is the issue of differently situated people. For example, if you earn less, you will pay less in taxes. Does this mean that you will be less of a citizen than someone with a higher salary will? What about those with less time due to working multiple jobs, be that wage labor or the second shift of unpaid caretaking and other familial duties. A composite picture is necessary to ensure a sense of rootedness. However, the forms of performing citizenship are potentially so multifaceted that it can be achieved in a variety of ways. For example, the act of caring for one's family *is* a contribution to the shared community. Similarly, paying more in taxes than does someone else does not speak to a greater level of engagement—only a higher tax bracket.

A related issue is, if citizenship is predicated on one's performance, whether someone can lose citizenship when they stop performing. Examples of this situation might include someone with dual citizenship residing in another country, hermits who do not take part in social engagement, and coma patients.[2] In the first case, it could be argued that those with dual citizenship benefit from a paper-based— not performance-based—citizenship as they retain citizenship in both countries while, potentially, only sharing in the common life of the community in which they reside. However, a person with dual citizenship can be performing citizenship in both countries. While not a dual citizen myself, it seems very possible to have that same sense of stewardship and shared fate in relation to multiple countries. I certainly feel that way towards multiple cities I have lived in—and it is a sense of loyalty that is not engendered while traveling. To deny someone citizenship because they no longer reside there seems to be relying on a Westphalian notion of exclusive citizenship instead of a more denationalized understanding. As for both the hermit and the coma patient, I would consider it fair to allow exceptions based on the special circumstances of individuals. Not everyone likes to, wants to, or can participate in social engagement. Similarly, an individual cannot be expected to do all—or even most—of the activities identified. For example, someone without children obviously cannot perform citizenship by raising the next generation. In general, there should be multiple performances that count, as well as a reasonable minimum. Performance-based citizenship is intended as a way to recognize, not deny, people's contributions.

The final concern relates to those who are just going through the motions of performing citizenship without actually feeling a sense of loyalty or a sense of shared fate with other members of the community. In this way, are performances like time in residence; intended to be a proxy for something deeper, but unable to be truly measured? This may, indeed, be the case. I do not pretend to know what lurks within people's hearts. However, would communities be any worse off if not everyone that contributed did so from a pure heart? A volunteer may not want to be sorting toys for tots—may not believe that children should get toys, may not support the marines, may not endorse the celebration of Christmas—but the toys get sorted all the same. This may sound like court-ordered community service. However, is this any different from other pragmatic or instrumental reasons for applying for citizenship? For the minority of people that may be acting in bad faith, there are many more who would finally be recognized for the contributions they are already making, and who do not now have the option of applying for citizenship under the current system.

*****

In this chapter, I have argued for us to flip our understandings of political obligation. Instead of the goods of the state triggering obligations on the part of the citizenry to carry out certain duties, the carrying out of those duties—performing citizenship—obligates the state to protect the individual and provide certain goods. The type of performances that would trigger state obligation needs to come from a rooted position, be sustained over time, and provide contributions to the larger social scheme.

However, determining what specific activities constitute performing citizenship is still vague. As much as we intuitively understand what it means to be engaged in a shared life and contribute to a cooperative scheme, it is a different matter to create policies that recognize such performances. Carens, facing a similar dilemma, acknowledged that he could not assess the political feasibility of his arguments, but noted that "Nevertheless I judged it appropriate for me to focus here on what I think is the right course in principle and leave to others the important task of judging how we might need to modify that course to take account of political realities" (Carens 1998, 146). I would like to claim a similar caveat and a theorist's prerogative to discuss ethical obligations and theoretical bases, even while acknowledging the difficulty of crafting institutional solutions.

Practical limitations acknowledged, I did still want to investigate policy implications and the political feasibility of a performance-based conception of citizenship. To that end, I researched policy makers' debates surrounding state legislation. I wanted to see how public officials conceptualized forms of citizenship and articulated resulting obligations, if any, on the part of the state. In the next two chapters, I turn to policies intended to extend certain privileges to undocumented residents—namely, driving and paying an in-state tuition rate at public universities. I examine the arguments made both for and against these policies in order to analyze the ways in which group membership is constructed. That is, when are undocumented members of the community seen as "us," part of "we, the people," and, therefore, deserving of state protections and entitlements.

Notes

1 Illinois Senate transcript, 5/7/2003, 22.
2 I would like to thank participants in the Political Theory Group at University of California, Irvine, for raising these scenarios.

References

Carens, Joseph H. 2013. *The Ethics of Immigration*. New York: Oxford University Press.
———. 2009. "The Case for Amnesty." *Boston Review*, Vol. 34, No. 3 (May/June), 1–13.
———. 1998. "Why Naturalization Should Be Easy: A Response to Noah Pickus." In *Immigration and Citizenship in the Twenty-First Century*,

edited by Noah M. J. Pickus, 141–146. Lanham, MD: Rowman & Little-field Publishers, Inc.

Cohen, Elizabeth. 2015. "The Political Economy of Immigrant Time: Rights, Citizenship, and Temporariness in the Post-1965 Era." *Polity*, Vol. 47, No. 3 (July), 337–351.

DeLue, Steven M. 1989. *Political Obligation in a Liberal State.* Albany: State University of New York Press.

Gilbert, Margaret. 2008. *A Theory of Political Obligation.* New York: Oxford University Press.

Green, T. H. 1986. "Lectures on the Principles of Political Obligation." In *Lectures on the Principles of Political Obligation and Other Writings*, edited by Paul Harris and John Morrow, 13–193. Cambridge: Cambridge University Press.

Gutmann, Amy. 1993. "The Challenge of Multiculturalism in Political Ethics." *Philosophy and Public Affairs*, Vol. 22, No. 3 (Summer), 171–206.

Horton, John. 2010. *Political Obligation*, 2nd edition. New York: Palgrave Macmillan.

Klosko, George. 2011. "Are Political Obligations Content Independent?" *Political Theory*, Vol. 39, No. 4 (August), 498–523.

———. 2009. "Cosmopolitanism, Political Obligation, and the Welfare State." *Political Theory*, Vol. 37, No. 2 (April), 243–265.

———. 2005. *Political Obligations.* New York: Oxford University Press.

———. 2004. "Multiple Principles of Political Obligation." *Political Theory*, Vol. 32, No. 6 (December), 801–824.

Kymlicka, Will. 1995. *Multicultural Citizenship: A Liberal Theory of Minority Rights.* Oxford: Clarendon Press.

Locke, John. 1980 [1690]. *Second Treatise of Government*, edited by C. B. Macpherson. Indianapolis, IN: Hackett Publishing Company, Inc.

Macedo, Stephen. 2007. "The Moral Dilemma of U.S. Immigration Policy: Open Borders Versus Social Justice?" In *Debating Immigration*, edited by Carol M. Swain, 63–81. Cambridge: Cambridge University Press.

Marshall, T. H. 1950. *Citizenship and Social Class.* Cambridge: Cambridge University Press.

Parekh, Bhikhu. 1993. "A Misconceived Discourse on Political Obligation." *Political Studies*, Vol. 41, No. 2 (June), 236–251.

Pateman, Carole. 1985. *The Problem of Political Obligation: A Critique of Liberal Theory.* Berkeley: University of California Press.

Pickus, Noah. 2005. *True Faith and Allegiance: Immigration and American Civic Nationalism.* Princeton, NJ: Princeton University Press.

Riley, Patrick. 1982. *Will and Political Legitimacy: A Critical Exposition of Social Contract Theory in Hobbes, Locke, Rousseau, Kant and Hegel.* Cambridge: Harvard University Press.

Simmons, John. 1981. *Moral Principles and Political Obligations.* Princeton: Princeton University Press.

Wolff, Robert Paul. 1998. *In Defense of Anarchism.* Berkeley: University of California Press.

4 Dare to DREAM

State-Level Versions
of the DREAM Act

> This bill acknowledges that the young people affected by it are
> Americans in every sense but for that piece of paper. They have
> grown up here. They have played little league with our children.
> They've sat side by side with our children in class. They are Ameri-
> cans and we owe them the same opportunity all of our children
> have.
>
> —Representative Claire Levy (Democrat)[1]

Representative Levy, in arguing for passage of the Colorado version of the DREAM Act, relied precisely on what I have termed
performance-based citizenship rather than using our current legal
conception of citizenship based solely on documents. She makes the
claim that undocumented students *are* Americans based on rootedness in their communities, acting in a way similar to other American
children, and participating in community-building activities such as
Little League. In turn, these characteristics and activities—repeatedly
performing citizenship—lead to specific obligations on the part of
lawmakers to provide similar opportunities to citizen-performing
individuals as those provided to other citizens.

The opportunity advocated for by Representative Levy in the
above epigraph is tuition equity, in which undocumented residents
are granted in-state tuition rates at public universities. This chapter
takes such state-level tuition equity proposals—often called DREAM
Acts—as an informative example of states extending certain benefits
or privileges to undocumented residents. The multiple debates that
have occurred in legislatures across the county about this issue provide
a rich discussion of what constitutes citizenship and when obligations
are owed to those who are American in every way but on paper. As we
will see, the arguments put forth by proponents of such policies echo

my theory that performing citizenship triggers obligations on the part of the state to undocumented members of the polity. That is, those who fulfill the duties of citizenship—paying taxes, engaged in their communities, contributing to a shared life—are owed certain protections and entitlements from the state, regardless of whether they have been authorized by the nation-state.

State-Level DREAM Acts

At the time of this writing, 20 states offer in-state tuition to undocumented students.[2] Such state-level action comes in response to the federal government's inability to pass the Development, Relief, and Education for Alien Minors Act. The federal DREAM Act has been (unsuccessfully) proposed in Congress every year since 2001. If passed, the act would provide a path to citizenship for individuals who came to the United States before the age of 16, as long as they have resided in the United States at least five years and either attended college or enlisted in the military for two years. In addition, an applicant can be disqualified if they commit a crime, are likely to become a public charge, or lack good moral character. The definition of good moral character has not been enumerated in any of the various versions of the DREAM Act. However, the Immigration and Naturalization Act (INA) includes being a habitual drunkard or gambler as examples of what might be considered poor moral character.[3]

It should be noted that, as discussed in Chapter Three, these requirements reflect our intuitions about what is necessary to be considered a citizen. In addition to amount of time in residence, the individual must show a contribution to society through military service or the promise of future contributions through a college education. In addition, someone worthy of citizenship would not be a criminal, dependent on the system, or morally challenged. Both the DREAM Act and the Deferred Action for Childhood Arrivals program require that the applicant arrived in the United States as a minor, thus mitigating her legal responsibility. This claim of blamelessness in the process of migration and, therefore, increased desert will be discussed in greater detail below. However, the other requirements of time, societal contributions, and lack of bad behavior parallel the actions of performing citizenship, while having the extra benefit of being able to be proven through various records. A broader conception of performance-based citizenship would be harder to prove, but would also recognize rootedness and engagement in the community over time and an expanded understanding of societal contributions that would allow more people to be recognized than those able to attend college or willing to risk their life by joining the military.

If the federal DREAM Act is ever enacted, and an individual were to meet the specified criteria, she would be granted conditional nonimmigration status. After nine years as a legal nonimmigrant, the individual would be eligible to apply for an adjustment of status to become a permanent legal resident, and, after three more years, could apply for naturalized citizenship. The major focus of the federal DREAM Act is also the key difference between the federal legislation and state-level versions; that is, providing a path to citizenship. State-level acts do not have the power to defer deportation or adjust an individual's immigration status. However, what both federal and state-level DREAM Acts do provide is the ability to pay an in-state tuition rate. Without this legislation, undocumented students have to pay the much higher rate that out-of-state and international students pay, regardless of the fact that many DREAMers have lived in the state for most of their lives.

The difference in tuition rates is not a small matter, with out-of-state students typically paying three to four times more than do state residents. The basis for the justification of providing discounted tuition rates to residents is that they and their families have been paying state and local taxes that, in turn, provide funding to the state colleges and universities. In contrast, those living out of state have not been paying into the public coffers. Similar to in-state residents, undocumented students and their families have also been paying state and local taxes. Thus, for the justification to be consistent—that is, that those paying into the pool of money used to subsidize public schools should pay less when attending those schools—undocumented residents should be given the discounted rate.

Another argument for the passage of both the federal and state-level DREAM Acts is that primary education is extended to all minors in the United States regardless of legal status. *Plyler v. Doe*, a 1982 Supreme Court case, prohibited states from excluding undocumented children from public education. Supporters of the DREAM Act argue that, given this right to primary education, it is not fair to then deprive students access to secondary education. In addition, one of the major incentives to do well in high school is to get into college. If college is not an option, there is less reason to strive for excellence in K–12. The United States, it is argued, should encourage capable students to take the next step in the education process. It is through their productivity and accomplishments that the United States will reap the investment of funding primary education. To cut off someone at the point of college education—and potentially deport them—is to lose the money and time already invested in them. Supporters also point out that the DREAM Act focuses on those immigrants most likely to have higher levels of income in the future and, therefore, pay more taxes. It is exactly those educated and productive members of society that will contribute more to the United States than they will take (in the form of social services).

State-based DREAM Acts vary from state to state. However, there are certain commonalities. The acts consistently require that the individual in question has attended a state high school for a set amount of years (ranging from two to four depending on the state), has graduated from a state high school or received a General Educational Development credential (GED), and is willing to sign an affidavit claiming that he/she will file for legal immigration status as soon as eligible to do so. The eligibility referenced in the latter requirement depends on the federal government changing immigration laws or offering some form of amnesty to those residing in the United States without nation-state authorization. Thus, there is a chance that those students signing the affidavit may never, in fact, be eligible to apply for legal status.

The reason that state-level DREAM Acts require high school attendance instead of residence is in order to comply with federal law. Section 1623 of the Immigration and Nationality Act provides that:

> Notwithstanding any other provision of law, an alien who is not lawfully present in the United States shall not be eligible on the basis of residence within a State (or a political subdivision) for any postsecondary education benefit unless a citizen or national of the United States is eligible for such a benefit (in no less an amount, duration, and scope) without regard to whether the citizen or national is such a resident.[4]

As a result of this provision, states must avoid using residence as the basis for tuition equity criteria if they wish to offer undocumented residents in-state tuition without eliminating the fiscally beneficial out-of-state tuition designation. Hence, states have adopted the requirement that a student must have attended a high school in the state for at least a minimum amount of time.

The California version of the DREAM Act was legally challenged in *Martinez v. Regents of the University of California* (2010) with the claim that it violated the Immigration and Nationality Act. The Court found in California's favor, upholding the law, due to the fact that in-state tuition was granted based on criteria other than residence; namely, attending a high school within the state's borders. The University of California's Board of Regents provided three examples of nonresident citizens that met the criteria and, therefore, were eligible for the in-state tuition rate. First, students living in adjoining states are sometimes permitted to attend California high schools. Second, students who attended boarding school in California while still legal dependents of parents living in other states are considered nonresidents. Finally, students that attended three years of high school in California but moved away for their senior year could still qualify for the lower rate. The *Martinez* decision was often referenced during debates about tuition equity bills in other states and used as an assurance that the proposed bill would not violate federal law.

Analyzing the Legislative Debates Over State-Level DREAM Acts

Tuition equity bills provide an example of an often contentious—but increasingly successful—policy in which states are extending privileges to undocumented members of their communities. The ensuing debates offer insight into how such an extension of privileges was justified. In order to analyze the arguments surrounding these policy proposals, I amassed legislative transcripts—be that written copies, videos, or audio files—covering roll call votes, floor debates, public hearings, and/or congressional meetings related to the prospective bills. I then identified patterns of arguments, focusing especially on how underlying conceptions of citizenship and community were used to either support or oppose the statutes. That is, who was deemed part of the group to whom lawmakers owed consideration? Was the membership limited to those with nation-state authorization or did it also include those performing citizenship?

I focus on two policy areas in this book: tuition equity and driver authorization cards. Both policies affect state residents that are not authorized by the federal government. However, the benefits provided by state-based DREAM Acts are limited to young people who are presumably bright and motivated to attend college. In addition, the rhetoric surrounding this issue paints the potential beneficiaries as blameless, perhaps even victims of their parents' act of irregular migration. Conversely, in the next chapter, I cover states proposing to make driver authorization cards available to all residents, not just the "innocent children" of the DREAMer narrative. Thus, we see differences in the two policy debates in regard to the characteristics of the individual in question, as well as potential contributions the individual may provide society. However, similar themes emerge which reveal underlying questions about *what* the state owes, *why*, and to *whom*. Consistent with my central argument, those themes suggest that the state does, indeed, have important obligations to those who effectively perform citizenship, regardless of their legal status.

Obligations of the State

Debates surrounding state-level DREAM Acts often included discussions regarding the role of political representatives and the obligations of the state. New York Senator Stewart-Cousins (Democrat), for example, thanked her fellow senators at the end of a floor debate for "standing and explaining and proclaiming and reminding us of our responsibility."[5] However, lawmakers differed in their perceptions about what their responsibility was and to whom it was owed. In this sense, the legislative debates offer an informative glimpse into how lawmakers grapple with the central question of the book: what, if anything, does the state owe undocumented residents who effectively perform citizenship?

Given the nature of the policy, tuition equity for higher education, there was much discussion about the state's obligation to provide access to education, referred to as "one of the state's paramount duties."[6] Some representatives attempted to frame the issue entirely in terms of education. For example, one Republican member of the Tennessee House of Representatives, Mark White, argued, "[t]his is about education, not about any sort of immigration reform."[7] However, even if there was consensus about the responsibility to provide access to education, representatives disagreed on the group of people to whom this responsibility was owed exactly because of immigration status.

If legislators only represent documented citizens—as many believe—then their "paramount duty" of providing access to education does not extend to noncitizens. When seen in this way, allowing undocumented students similar benefits denigrates the rights of the representatives' constituents. Thus, the duty of the state may be, in fact, to protect citizen students from these policies that, according to some, take away competitive admission slots and provide "lower costs to undocumented students [by] being subsidized by other students."[8] In this understanding, even though undocumented students and their families have paid taxes that subsidize the education of in-state students, they should not also benefit because their legal status bars them from being part of the political community to whom lawmakers are responsible. The "to whom obligation is owed" question leads to very different answers which, in turn, leads to divisions on these policy issues. Given these divisions, successful policy proposals must provide a convincing account as to why undocumented residents should be considered a member of the group to whom political obligations are owed.

Another obligation of the state often discussed in DREAM Act debates involved providing a voice to members of the public. New York State Assembly Speaker Heastie (Democrat), while discussing a bill that would allow undocumented students access to state financial aid, described part of his job during one of those sessions as ensuring "that the voices of even the most vulnerable among us can reach the highest levels of state government."[9] This sentiment echoes a statement made by his predecessor, Sheldon Silver, when lamenting the legislature's failure to pass the same bill a year before. Silver first argued that the refusal to pass the bill was "blatantly unfair to the thousands of talented, ambitious young New Yorkers who are being denied a college education, simply because of their immigration status." He then proceeded to promise to "work to make sure that the voices of these students—who know no other homeland—are heard loud and clear."[10] Thus, for both Heastie and Silver, undocumented residents *were* part of their constituents, which, in turn, led to the obligation to make sure their voices were heard.

The denial of financial aid and representation based "simply" on immigration status, however, does not strike all as "blatantly unfair." In fact, some argue that it is absolutely necessary to deny recognition of undocumented residents' voices in order to ensure that citizens' voices are adequately heard. For example, when talking about citizens who are opposed to the bill, Oregon Representative Conger (Republican) shared his concern "about what [passing a state-level DREAM Act] says to them about whether or not their voices are considered relevant by the legislature."[11] Colorado Senator Baumgardner (Republican) saw similar limitations regarding voice and recognition of citizens. He argued that his obligation was not to the undocumented residents of his state. "I represent Colorado citizens," the Senator stated, "I feel like we need to represent *legal* Colorado citizens."[12] Premising the state's obligation on paper citizenship, therefore, once again results in very different responsibilities and concerns than would be generated using my performance-based metric.

Another potential argument for why tuition equity is not the responsibility of state lawmakers—in addition to claiming legislators' obligations are limited to state citizens—is that immigration is a federal issue. This, consequently, leads to concerns that state laws will be pre-empted by federal court decisions striking down the respective legislation for violating federal law or encroaching on an area considered within the federal domain. One especially high-profile example, which garnered considerable media coverage, was the Justice Department's legal challenge to several provisions of Arizona's Senate Bill 1070. This controversial bill, passed in 2010, attempted to alter federal immigration law by, among other things, declaring that the failure to carry proper papers would now be a crime in Arizona, even though it is not a crime under federal law. The alteration of immigration law in this way was seen as a usurpation of federal power in a decidedly federal realm and was declared void by a federal court.

However, the Supreme Court has drawn a distinction between immigration regulation (e.g., determining legal status or penalties for violation of immigration law) and regulating immigrants (state laws relating to residents such as labor laws). In *DeCanas v. Bica* (1976), the Court reasoned that

> [p]ower to regulate immigration is unquestionably exclusively a federal power. But the Court has never held that every state enactment which in any way deals with aliens is a regulation of immigration and thus per se pre-empted by this constitutional power, whether latent or exercised.
>
> (424 U.S. 351, 355)

As a result, the states are left certain leeway when it comes to laws that only impact their residents, but must be wary of crossing into the federal domain of immigration regulation.

The necessity, discussed above, for states to base criteria for in-state tuition rates on attending high school instead of residency reflects these concerns. However, beyond that caveat, the state legislative debates did not include warnings of misplaced entry into a federal domain. That is, while there was a slight concern about federal pre-emption of the law if passed, there was no trepidation about violating the separation of powers by taking on a federal function. Instead, state legislators often talked about the state's obligation to take care of issues the federal government seemed unable or unwilling to accomplish. For example, New York Senator Peralta (Democrat) described state policy as an opportunity "to do something that the federal government has not been able to do."[13] Tennessee Representative White (Republican) was not as optimistic, viewing the need for states to get involved more as an unwanted responsibility than an opportunity. Or, as he put it:

> As a conservative Republican, I get it. But we are in a unique situation. Our federal government has messed up. They have allowed people to come in and they are victims, too.[14]

Oregon Representative Esquivel (Republican) was even less forgiving in asking: "Why are we in this situation in the first place? Because the federal government can't do their job."[15] Many lawmakers, in fact, argued that states were obligated to fill the void left by Washington D.C.'s paralysis on this issue. Several legislators suggested that the federal government's failure to provide comprehensive immigration reform has led not only to newfound responsibilities on the part of the states, but also to a potential reason the state may owe certain obligations to undocumented residents. That is, these state residents were victims of a broken immigration system and state lawmakers were responsible for mitigating the casualties.

If these legislators are correct that the state has obligations to provide access to education and recognize the voices of those they represent—that is, that these responsibilities are, in fact, state obligations—the remaining questions are to *whom* they owe these obligations and *why*. In other words, are these obligations owed to noncitizens and, if federally granted citizenship is no longer the determination of who is owed consideration, what is? My theory argues that obligations are owed to those performing citizenship—those who are engaged in their communities, with a sense of shared fate, and contributing to the larger collaborative arrangement necessary for a shared life. But are those arguments reflected in the legislative debates about what the state owes to its undocumented residents?

To Whom Is the Obligation Owed?

> I've come to ask why we want to visit the sins of the father on
> their children. I've come to ask why I would close out hope for
> a productive life while these children wait for irrational laws to
> change.
>
> —Representative Max Tyler (Democrat)[16]

The general, underlying question that I answer in this book was also
front and center in legislative debates about state-level immigration
policies that extend benefits to undocumented immigrants. That is,
to whom are these obligations owed? Representative Tyler, quoted
above, provided two reasons that are often put forth by proponents
of state-level DREAM Acts: the faulty federal immigration system
and the innocence of the potential beneficiaries. I will take each
of these in turn before then proceeding to arguments that provide
pictures of performing citizenship.

   We are often reminded that the United States is a nation of
immigrants. This sentiment was as popular in state houses as it
is in public discourse. Many hours of debate were dedicated to
recounting the voyages of parents and grandparents from the
old country to the gleaming shores of Ellis Island. Such accounts
were often followed with the seemingly inevitable achievement
of the American dream earned through hard work. However,
this often led to legislators making the claim that their ancestors had migrated legally, thus providing justification for not
including more recent groups of migrants into the United States
melting pot. In fact, some saw their migrant ancestry as reason to
fight against the extension of benefits to those who remain in the
United States without proper authorization. Representative Saine
(Republican), for instance, claimed that she opposed the Colorado
DREAM Act because it "wrongs generations of immigrants that
came here legally."[17] Similarly, Saine's colleague in the Senate,
Senator Lundberg (Republican), took umbrage with the claim that
undocumented Colorado students should be considered members
in the nation of immigrants. "It's not people who have immi-
grated," he clarified, "it's people who have come here illegally."[18]
In this way, the communities are separated into those who help
build the nation and those who potentially destroy it—us and
other. The first group is deserving of consideration, the second
group is not.

   In response to this line of argument, proponents of state tuition
equity bills pointed to the changing immigration regimes that have

led to increasingly restrictive policies. Immigration laws have illegalized behavior that was once accepted and is still encouraged. The patchwork of federal laws have more often been passed in reaction to the public's mislaid fear or in reaction to other political situations—such as the preferred status granted to Cuban migrants—than through a thoughtful, logical, holistic process. Thus, as I argued in Chapter One, shifts in federal immigration policy may be a reason that undocumented members of our communities are owed more than we currently claim.

Many representatives talked about the desire of their constituents to become citizens, only to be met with long wait times and high costs. As a Washington Bill Report explains, "Immigration laws often function as a barrier to these students becoming documented. Many families spend thousands of dollars and many years and still struggle with legal status."[19] Some arguments focused on the similar motivations of earlier generations and the same desire to work hard to achieve a better life. New York Senator Klein (Democrat), for example, claimed there was no difference "between the prior immigration generation and those who come here today . . . They're all the same. They come to make America their home. They come to make a better life for them and their family."[20] Others took a slightly different approach, reminding their colleagues that what has changed is federal policy, not the merit of the migrants. Senator Parker (Democrat) used these shifting policies as a reason justifying the inclusion of undocumented students into the "citizenry" that the state is obligated to help, arguing:

I think we don't understand how important it is to educate our citizenry no matter what the circumstances are in which they come here. But as we come and talk about the circumstances in which our folks have come here, we should be clear that what people's grandparents and great-grandparents did in order to become naturalized, let's not act like it's the same process, because it's not. Right? Because what people are doing now to become citizens is very, very different than writing your name as you got off a boat.[21]

Drawing attention to changing federal policies, therefore, shifts the image of the "illegal immigrant" to someone who, in a different time, would be lauded for having the courage and ambition to move to a new county.

The attempt to reframe the image of the undocumented resident from illegal to innocent was reflected in other arguments used by proponents of state-level DREAM Acts, thus leading to the "innocent child" defense. An individual may be faultless, and therefore deserving, if the blame lies with federal immigration policy and/ or with the parents who brought the individual to the United States when merely a child. A Washington State Senate Bill Report included the following argument for their tuition equity bill:

> This bill will provide that college opportunity for students who have attended and graduated from our high schools and proven themselves but cannot afford to continue their education because, *through no fault of their own*, they are waiting to attain legal status. These families have tried for a long time to gain citizenship and spent a lot of money but are still waiting.[22]

The phrase "through no fault of their own" is often used in arguments for both the federal and state-level DREAM Acts. Typically, it follows an account of how the individual migrated—the unauthorized act from which her current "illegal" status is derived. The premise of this argument is that potential beneficiaries of the program were innocent children when they were brought into the country by their parents, through no fault of their own. They, therefore, are not responsible for breaking immigration laws and deserve equal consideration to that given citizen students or, at least, more consideration than their parents.

   This idea of the innocent child—and therefore deserving recipient—is a popular argument in both floor debates and public discourse. The recurring theme is that the potential students are not "calculating adults who came to this country."[23] They are, instead, "children whose parents brought them to our country without proper documentation and no fault of their own."[24] While this characterization has been successful, it creates a set of problematic dichotomies. If the potential students are innocent, then their parents are guilty. If the children are deserving beneficiaries, their parents and other family members are not. These dichotomies open the door to "us versus them" rhetoric in a way that more inclusive arguments do not. It is, in fact, the more inclusive arguments—reflecting an expansive notion of performance-based citizenship—that led to even greater support for state legislation than that of the "innocent child."

   Opponents of state-based DREAM Acts rejected the image of the faultless minor, focusing instead on the action committed "through no fault of their own." Why, indeed, would anyone need to claim that the DREAMers were faultless unless there was something for which to be guilty? Thus, the attempt to mitigate guilt by using the "innocent child" argument put the focus on the initial act of migration instead of on the repeated activities carried out by these individuals as they perform citizenship. As a result, the most common opposition argument in legislative debates focused on the law-breaking acts of migration and presence in the state without nation-state authorization. Within this frame, the migrant was not deserving by nature of their illicit activity. "Illegal" immigrants were then pitted against the deserving group—be that taxpayers, other students vying for university spots, or legal immigrants that had gone through the process.

For some, lack of intention did not mitigate guilt or in any way alter the individual's desert. As Senator Engel (Democrat) explained, "I just have a very difficult time in promoting and/or condoning in-state tuition for anybody that's illegal. . . . illegal is illegal."[25] Similarly, Senator Cunningham (Republican) stated, "I'm very adamantly opposed to this bill and it comes down to the word 'illegal.' And I don't believe we should reward 'illegal' in any way."[26] In addition, opponents observed that the "innocent children" were now adults. In Tennessee's unsuccessful attempt to pass a DREAM Act, Representative Ragon (Republican) met the repetitive use of "through no fault of their own" with the following retort: "These people in your bill are no longer minors. Therefore, the decision to stay in this country is not their parents, but theirs."[27] Repeatedly, the "innocent child" argument opened the door to these type of rebuttals in a way that inclusive arguments—those referring to *our* children and members of *our* community—did not.

How, though, can opponents be convinced that undocumented residents are, in fact, members of our communities—even our political communities—and therefore deserving of our consideration and state obligation? In their viewpoint, citizenship and the resulting benefits are predicated on documents, not on performing the actions of a citizen. A case needs to be made for a broader understanding of citizenship and the extension of corollary protections and benefits. Lawmakers did exactly that with inclusive arguments that focused on contributions to the state and society—the cooperative scheme necessary to sustain a shared life—and rootedness in their communities. In other words, they made the case for performing citizenship.

What Are the Contributions and Characteristics That Trigger State Obligations?

If an individual's contributions are going to be considered, and even result in the state owing certain obligations to that individual, we must determine what actions and characteristics count. As discussed in the previous chapter, citizenship-like duties and actions are notoriously hard to articulate. One of the easiest contributions to quantify is the paying of taxes. This is the case in theoretical notions of political obligation, but is also a practically important component in justifying the extension of financial benefits. For example, as previously discussed, the justification for in-state tuition rates is premised on paying state taxes that, in turn, are used to fund public universities. It should be noted that DREAM Act proponents claim that there is no additional outlay of funds as the students would not be able to afford college at out-of-state rates. As a result, they argue, the universities will actually receive more money in tuition as tuition equity policies allow access to a greater group of students. Regardless of the direct link between taxes and the cost of the proposed policy, the paying of taxes is an important way that residents contribute to the shared fate of the community.

There is a widely held misperception that undocumented residents do not pay taxes. As a result, there were many speeches that included facts and figures about taxes paid. For example, Senator Peralta (Democrat) provided the following evidence on the floor of the New York Senate:

> In 2010, undocumented immigrants in this great state of ours paid $744,276,000 in taxes. And when you look at the federal level, every single year the Social Security Administration keeps $6 billion to $7 billion in Social Security contributions from W-2s that cannot be matched and the vast majority of that money comes from the undocumented immigrants. In the United States of America alone, undocumented [sic] paid $10.6 billion in state and local taxes.[28]

California Assembly Member Firebraugh (Democrat) made the direct link between paying taxes and resulting benefits. "These students and their families pay taxes and invest in the system; therefore," he asked, "should they not, in return, receive benefits?"[29] Similarly, a Washington State Senate Bill Report described their version of the DREAM Act as "a matter of justice and equity for

those people in our state who do pay taxes and who have contributed greatly to our state."[30] The wording notably implies that while
paying taxes is an important contribution, it is not the only contribution undocumented residents make to their states.

The idea that paying taxes was a sign of membership in the community was not a universally held belief, however. Bill opponents,
even when stipulating that undocumented migrants are taxpayers,
still made a distinction between the people who were worthy of
receiving taxpayer money and those who were not. As Representative Pritchard (Republican) explained: "A lot of people feel they
shouldn't be spending their tax dollars for people that aren't citizens."[31] In this way, the community of taxpayers is separated from
the community of citizens, and the link between paying in and,
therefore, deserving payouts is severed. In this mindset, it does not
matter that documented and undocumented individuals alike pay
taxes. Those deserving of benefitting from the resulting funds are
limited to paper citizens.

While supporters of tuition equity viewed the paying of taxes as
one of the signs of active membership in the community, the opposition held to a more traditional notion of citizenship. They viewed
nation-state authorization as the dividing line between deserving
and not, between member and outsider. This led to a rather frus-
trated reaction from Colorado Representative Duran (Democrat). In
response to a colleague's earlier statement that paying taxes did not
make someone a Coloradan, she claimed, "if you believe that, then
no wonder you're against this entire bill because, for you, it's those
people—those undocumented families over there—they're not Coloradans . . . They're not Coloradans, they're someone else."[32] This
exchange displays the underlying divisions in how membership and
obligations are determined. For those who only acknowledge paper
citizenship, residents without nation-state authorization will never
be Coloradans—never part of the "us" deserving consideration—
they will always remain "someone else."

If paying taxes is an insufficient proxy for community membership, what other contributions might be considered? Similar to my
theory of performing citizenship, lawmakers made the argument
that contributing to society in a myriad of potential ways, acting
like other citizens (true performativity), and having roots in the
community should be considered markers of insider status. Senator
Giron (Democrat), in presenting the Colorado DREAM Act, made
the case that it would enable the state "to reward young people who
have played by the rules, have done everything we've asked and

have excelled . . . They are now going to be able to give back—go to college and give back—continue giving back to our communities."[33] Similarly, Oregon Senator Courtney (Democrat) claimed the bill was "for young people who simply want a chance . . . They have paid their dues. They have paid dues in this state. This is their state. They want to become even better citizens."[34] Courtney's statement reveals the belief that undocumented students *are* already citizens. Additionally, both Senators Giron and Courtney view a college education as an important step in allowing these individuals to continue to contribute to their communities, to become "even better citizens" as they perform their duty of supporting the collective scheme necessary to sustain a shared life among their fellow community members.

Arguments regarding such contributions were often spoken in the language of inclusion: our children, our fellow Californians, our people. Representative Salazar's (Democrat) following statement provides a compelling example of that language:

> This is the moment in time when the wisdom of this general assembly held that Colorado's *own* children, children who love this state, children who have given to our societal enlightenment, children who have contributed to our economy, were finally and fully recognized as something more than illegal or undocumented. . . . It is your historic affirmation that the equality of higher education access for children that have always ever been Coloradans is of supreme importance.[35]

In this argument, we see the acknowledgment that contributions— both economic and social (and as ambiguous as giving "to our societal enlightenment")—result in obligations on the part of the state to recognize those performing citizenship (Colorado's own children) and provide access to education.

It should be noted that Colorado faced an uphill battle as the passing of their DREAM Act was in direct violation of a 2006 law that had explicitly blocked undocumented migrants from receiving benefits, including in-state tuition. In spite of this, the tuition equity bill passed with two-thirds support in both houses of the state legislature. Colorado lawmakers used inclusive language more consistently than evidenced in other states' floor debates, hearings, and public statements. Examples include Representative Williams's (Democrat) statement: "This is about inclusiveness. It's about equality and it's about ensuring that *our* children have an opportunity to continue their life-long learning."[36] Similarly, Senator Kefalas (Democrat) claimed, "[t]hey are our neighbors . . . they are *our* young people."[37] Senator Johnston (Democrat), a former educator, went as far as to say that DREAMers "are the most American kids I've ever worked with."[38] Potential beneficiaries *are* part of the community, *are* us, and, through their actions, perform as Americans. As a result, they deserve equal opportunities as every other member of the community.

This strategy of inclusive, performance-based arguments has two noticeable advantages for proponents of tuition equity. First of all, it avoids the dichotomies and "othering" of the innocent child argument. Instead of being set apart from their family and seen as victims, the DREAMers are one of us. They share our activities, our dreams, our attempts to build a common life. This discursive framing leads directly to the second advantage. If undocumented individuals are recognized members of the community, the onus is on state representatives to prove why obligations are *not* owed to them. Hence, not passing tuition equity bills becomes about placing obstacles in the path of deserving citizenship-performers instead of extending benefits to undeserving and unauthorized lawbreakers. Utah Senator Stephenson (Republican) deployed this strategy when arguing, "[t]hey've attended the schools, they are part of the community . . . We're now barring them from continuing with their involvement in our community."[39] Within this perspective, instead of undocumented individuals seen as outsiders and interlopers destroying the American way of life, it is the states that are destroying communities by failing to recognize all of its members.

The proceedings in Illinois provide interesting insight into the impact of framing the debate using inclusive discourse. The state passed their version of the DREAM Act in 2003 with incredibly high levels of support. The arguments used at that time largely relied on notions of inclusion and community. For example, during the floor debate in the House, Representative Soto (Democrat) explained that the bill was "very important to our communities . . . all . . . all of our communities. Because they also come from our communities."[40] Likewise, Senator Sandoval (Democrat) stated: "We can no longer treat these students as strangers."[41] The only "no" vote in the Senate was Senator Lauzen (Republican), who saw the bill as benefiting "illegal" immigrants at the cost of citizens and encouraging future unauthorized immigration, two arguments that would gain traction in future debates.[42]

In 2011, the Illinois legislature passed Senate Bill 2185. While called the Illinois DREAM Act, it was merely an extension of the initial bill passed in 2003. The follow-up bill was modest in its intent, yet fiercely opposed. The bill created a scholarship fund to collect private donations for undocumented students, provided training for high school and college counselors to ensure they were aware of the college opportunities available to undocumented students, and allowed parents to invest their pretax income in either of the two state college savings programs.

The existing policy regarding in-state tuition was purportedly not up for debate; however, that was not the case. The resulting discussions were very much about extending benefits to undocumented students. Arguments in favor of the 2011 policy moved away from notions of inclusion and community and relied much more heavily on the image of the innocent child of law-breaking parents. As with other states, this opened the door to questions of innocence and responsibility that are avoided when arguments are framed, instead, in the discourse of inclusion. The resulting votes reflect the more divisive debate. The initial act providing for in-state tuition passed with 98% support in the Senate and 96% support in the house. The DREAM Act Fund bill, in contrast, garnered 80% support in the Senate and only 53% in the House. Of course, legislative votes do not happen in a vacuum. External factors may have influenced the drop in support from 2003 to 2011. However, the Illinois House and Senate were controlled by the Democratic Party in both years—so the most obvious potential cause for such a shift was not the case.

In all of the states analyzed, arguments for inclusion rested heavily on a premise of rootedness; that is, that the potential beneficiaries of the bills were deeply imbricated within the fabric of their society. Senator Hassell-Thompson (Democrat), in claiming that DREAMers are our children, explained "they only know America as their homeland. They only know New York as the place of their friendships, their relationships."[43] They are part of a web of networks within our cities and states. More importantly, they do not belong anywhere else. They are not migrants, which implies they are still in motion; they are members of our community.

The requirement of rootedness parallels the sustained performance required for performing citizenship and the understanding that something more is required than merely visiting or time in residence. This is evidenced in discussions about why it is justified to offer in-state tuition to undocumented residents but is not extended to, for example, international students. In a letter to Governor

O'Malley, then Attorney General of Maryland, Douglas F. Gansler, wrote:

> The entire purpose of the bill is to design a law that will enable the State to continue to provide services to young undocumented aliens, many of whom came here as children, have attended Maryland schools, and have an attachment to the State. It is not irrational to assume that nonimmigrant aliens here on a temporary basis have less of an attachment.[44]

Thus, once again, attachment—the tethering of social bonds—is used as a criterion for whom should be provided state services.

Attachments, roots, and acting American are also used as a way to ward against fears of terrorism. After 9/11, terrorism and immigration became linked in the public imagination. This is not without cause. Some of those involved in downing the planes were in the United States on expired visas. In addition, Immigration and Naturalization Services (INS) was replaced by Immigration Control and Enforcement (ICE), which was placed under the umbrella of the newly created Department of Homeland Security. Fears of terrorism play a much bigger role in debates about driver authorization cards, which is the subject of the next chapter. However, such fears were not absent from DREAM Act discourse. For example, when Kansas passed its version of the DREAM Act in 2004, Representative Schwab (Republican) registered his unhappiness with the explanation that "if terrorists come to get a pilot's license at a Kansas university, at least we gave them in-state tuition before they use it against us."[45] New York Senator Padavan (Republican) provided a similar note of caution in the following statement:

> The overwhelming percentage of these young people who are undocumented are of no danger to this country. But I suggest to you it only takes a few, as we found out, to be up to no good. At least we should know who they are, where they're coming from, and what they're doing. The part of this bill that talks about having gone to high school here and all of that I have no problem with, because that identifies some roots.[46]

As evidenced by his statement, Padavan accepts the idea of roots and attachments as a justification and argument against the fear of DREAMer terrorists. However, the same idea leads him to conclude that "all is well and good until you get to the last item, the

GED, which is a walk-in test."[47] Thus, his opposition to the bill was due to allowing a GED to serve as an alternative to attending high school exactly because he accepted the argument that attending high school in the state helped to build attachments and inculcate students into the American way of life.

Senator Mendez (Republican) mirrored this idea in her defense against fears of terrorism. "By the time these youngsters go to college," she claims "they already, they already have become very Americanized. Okay? So they do not present a danger."[48] Attending schools and being educated alongside citizens helps the assimilation process. It also helps to habituate the individual into performing citizenship: pledging allegiance to the American flag, learning the history, and planning for a shared future.

It was successfully argued in 20 states that undocumented residents—described as contributors, rooted in our communities, even citizens—were owed in-state tuition. However, it was not lost on opponents that citizen privileges were being extended and, in fact, were being done so through an expansion of the definition of citizen. In the first case, Kansas Representative Vickbey (Republican) stated, "I strongly oppose affording illegal immigrants the same rights and privileges of children of our own tax-paying Kansas citizens."[49] To the second point, Senator Grissanti (Republican) clarified that "enacting the DREAM Act does not convey citizenship on an individual."[50] The fact that Senator Grissanti felt this needed to be said highlights that others believe exactly that—or, at least, that those to whom tuition equity is due may also be owed other rights and privileges.

In an impassioned speech, Utah Senator Hickman (Republican) provided the following defense of nation-state citizenship:

> What I am concerned about is for those individuals that have gone through the process to become citizens of this country in order that they can enjoy the benefits of citizenship and enjoy the freedoms that go along with citizenship and privileges and all the other things that being a citizen of this great country affords. I think there's value there. It doesn't matter what color your skin is. It doesn't matter what language you speak. It doesn't matter what religion you might practice. But it does matter to me that I'm a citizen of this country and I value that and I believe that in order for us to be able to enjoy the privileges that go along with being a citizen of this country we have responsibilities—we have responsibilities to meet our

obligations to support this country, to stand by it, to be willing to fight for it. We also have a responsibility to pay our taxes and all the other things that go along with citizenship. What I don't agree with is that we're allowing those privileges to be eroded.[51]

I quote Senator Hickman in some length here because he captures both the fear and the promise of what I argue for in this book. He lists the various responsibilities of citizenship—those activities that constitute the performance of citizenship—and he does so in the language of political obligation. According to Hickman, it is because of the benefits and freedoms of citizenship that we owe certain obligations to support the country. As I have argued, those who meet the responsibilities listed—stand by one's country, be willing to fight for it, pay your taxes—should be provided the privileges of citizenship. Hickman realizes that this is exactly what happened with the Utah DREAM Act. He sees it as an erosion of citizen's rights. I see it as a consequence of honoring those performing citizenship.

*****

In this chapter, I have explored arguments surrounding state-level tuition equity bills. In these debates, we see lawmakers grappling with questions about what the state owes, to whom these obligations are owed, and why. If the group to be considered—the group to whom obligations are owed—is limited by nation-state authorization, the state has a parochial duty to protect them and limit access to opportunities to only those with paper citizenship. In the case of state-level DREAM Acts, this means making sure that in-state tuition is only granted to citizens and ensuring that the voices recognized and represented in the legislature are limited to those with nation-state authorization.

If, however, the group to be considered is determined by different criteria—thus changing the justification for why an individual is owed obligations—the group membership changes and the state is now obligated to provide access and recognition to the larger group. In discussing the new criteria to be considered, lawmakers relied on such characteristics as being rooted in the community, contributing socially and economically, and planning for a future for the individual and the state. In this, we see an articulation of what constitutes the performances of citizenship.

It was, in fact, arguments based on community belonging and the sustained and future activities of the individuals—contributing to the larger collective scheme necessary for a shared life—that met with less opposition than those that relied on the image of the DREAMer as an innocent child brought to the United States through no fault of her own. Thus, a focus on performing citizenship proved to be more successful in arguing for the desert of potential beneficiaries than an attempt to mitigate blame for their initial unauthorized entry into the country. We also see lawmakers recognizing that those who effectively perform citizenship are entitled to certain privileges in return. Thus, the carrying out of civic duties triggers state obligations and a group once rendered invisible is seen, recognized, and heard through performing citizenship.

Notes

1 Colorado State House of Representatives floor debate, March 8, 2013.
2 California, Colorado, Connecticut, Florida, Illinois, Kansas, Maryland, Minnesota, Nebraska, New Jersey, New Mexico, New York, Oregon, Texas, Utah, and Washington did so through their state legislatures. Hawaii, Michigan, Oklahoma, and Rhode Island enacted similar policies through their state university governing boards. Percentage of support for the bills by state and chamber can be found in Appendix A.
3 U.S. Citizenship and Immigration Services, *Citizenship and Naturalization Policy Manual*. Accessed at http://www.uscis.gov/policymanual/HTML/PolicyManual-Volume12-PartF-Chapter5.html#S-I on 8/19/2015.
4 8 U.S.C. § 1623.
5 New York Senate floor debate for March 17, 2014.
6 Washington State House Bill Report on EHB 1079 (4/21/03).
7 Tennessee State House of Representatives transcripts (4/22/15).
8 Representative Everett (Republican), Colorado State House of Representatives (3/5/2013).
9 Remarks made by Assembly Speaker Carl E. Heastie, Speaker's Conference Room, Albany, New York (2/26/2015).
10 News Release from the desk of New York State Assembly Speaker Sheldon Silver (3/17/2014).
11 Oregon State House of Representatives floor debate for February 22, 2013.
12 Colorado State Senate floor debate for February 22, 2013.
13 New York State Senate floor debate for March 17, 2014.
14 Tennessee State House of Representatives transcripts for April 22, 2015.
15 Oregon State House of Representatives floor debate, February 22, 2013.
16 Colorado State House of Representatives floor debate, March 8, 2013.
17 Colorado House of Representatives floor debate for March 8, 2013.
18 Colorado Senate floor debate for February 22, 2013.
19 Washington State House Bill Report on EHB 1079 (4/21/2003). Similarly, Senator Oppenheimer claims, "I think the bottom line here is that many of these parents would love to become citizens, and I think the problem lies with our immigration service." New York State Senate floor debate, June 20, 2002.

20 New York State Senate floor debate, March 17, 2014.
21 New York State Senate floor debate, March 17, 2014. Another example was in New York Senator Stavisky's (Democrat) statement in which he argued "in the past 50 years or so [we] have had a totally different immigration policy than that which existed at that time. We have highly restrictive immigration laws. We have quotas. We have the McCarran-Walter Act. So it's a totally different concept." New York State Senate floor debate, March 17, 2014.
22 Washington State Senate Bill Report on EHB 1079 (3/27/2003). Emphasis is mine. Senator Hassell-Thompson used similar verbiage: "One of the things that concerns me a great deal is if these young people are accepted into our college institutions and are further penalized because, through no fault of their own, that because of paperwork, because of backlog in INS, that we are not able to facilitate their ability to pay in-state." New York State Senate floor debate, June 20, 2002.
23 Senator Looney (Democrat), Connecticut Senate transcripts for May 24, 2011, 248–9.
24 Representative Candelaria (Democrat), Connecticut House transcripts for May 12, 2011, 2. Other examples include Schimek (Democrat): "They were brought here by their parents. They are not criminals and they shouldn't be treated like criminals. They are children" (Nebraska Legislature transcripts, 4/11/2006, 13289). Cullerton (Democrat): "Now, we are talking about children, who perhaps didn't even choose to come to this country" (Illinois Senate transcript, 5/4/2011, 29). Dembrow (Democrat): "They did not choose to come here. They were brought here. They have no other country to go to" (Oregon State House floor debate, February 22, 2013).
25 Nebraska State Legislative transcript for April 11, 2006, 13276.
26 Nebraska State Legislative transcript for April 11, 2006, 13277.
27 Tennessee State House of Representatives transcript for April 22, 2015.
28 New York State Senate floor debate, March 17, 2014.
29 California Assembly Bill Analysis for AB 540, 9/13/2001.
30 Washington State Senate Bill Report on EHB 1079, 3/27/2003.
31 Illinois State House of Representatives transcripts for May 30, 2011, 177.
32 Colorado State House of Representatives floor debate, March 5, 2013.
33 Colorado State Senate floor debate, February 25, 2013.
34 Oregon State Senate floor debate, March 21, 2013.
35 Colorado State House of Representatives floor debate, March 8, 2013.
36 Colorado State House of Representatives floor debate, March 8, 2013.
37 Colorado State Senate floor debate, February 22, 2013.
38 Colorado State Senate floor debate, February 22, 2013.
39 Utah State Senate floor debate, February 28, 2002.
40 Illinois State House of Representatives transcript for March 5, 2003, 38.
41 Illinois State Senate transcript for May 7, 2003, 20.
42 Senator Lauzen (Republican):

> The issue of illegal immigrants having equal access to the limited spots in our State universities, as do children of legal citizens, is not just about money and about tuition; it's about who gets the

few precious spots that are available . . . Already, elementary and secondary education has been provided, and now there's another incentive if this bill passes, another incentive for folks to break the immigration law and to come illegally.

(Illinois Senate transcript, 5/7/2003, 14)

43 New York State Senate floor debate, March 17, 2014.
44 A letter from the Attorney General of Maryland, Douglas F. Gansler, to Governor Martin O'Malley regarding Maryland Senate Bill 167, dated May 9, 2011.
45 Kansas State House of Representatives transcripts for May 4, 2004.
46 New York State Senate transcripts for June 20, 2002.
47 Ibid.
48 New York State Senate floor debate, June 20, 2002.
49 Kansas State House of Representatives transcripts for May 4, 2004.
50 New York State Senate floor debate, March 17, 2014.
51 Utah State Senate floor debate, February 28, 2002.

5 Rights v. Privileges
Driver Authorization Cards

> We have roughly eleven and a half million illegal immigrants in the U.S., the overwhelming majority of whom are hard-working and actually pay taxes. The notion that a careful process to issue those few in Vermont with identification cards or driving cards will either affect immigration enforcement or threaten national security by its existence simply exalts fear over reason.
> —Representative Richard J. Marek (Democrat)[1]

In the previous chapter, I explored arguments surrounding state-level laws extending in-state tuition rates to undocumented residents of the state. While still meeting resistance, these policy proposals have become increasingly successful. As discussed earlier, state-level DREAM Acts are appealing to many because the beneficiaries of the policy are characterized as a limited group of highly successful young people who had no say in being brought to this county. In contrast, those who would benefit from driver authorization cards often include a much broader population. Many of these individuals actively chose to migrate and to remain in the state without legal documents. In addition, and to make matters worse for some, the undocumented residents may need a driver's license to drive to a job where they are employed without proper federal authorization.

Identification cards also incite concerns regarding terrorism with the fear that any state-issued form of identification may enable the card-bearer to board a plane—a hypothetical situation repeatedly used in debates to evoke images of 9/11. In addition, access to education—even higher education—is often viewed as a right. Driving, on the other hand, is often seen as a privilege, a benefit that can be denied. As a result, in debates surrounding driver authorization cards, a new set of frames and arguments emerge. Nevertheless,

Representative Marek's argument in the epigraph introducing this chapter reveals a similar call to recognize the contributions being made by undocumented members of our communities—contributions such as working and paying taxes—that he suggests may trigger certain considerations from the state.

In the same way that arguments in favor of state-level DREAM Acts reflected my conception of performance-based citizenship, proponents for driver authorization cards similarly relied on the need to recognize and include those who are fulfilling certain civic duties. Those involved in the debates described the activities performed by undocumented residents in terms similar to what we have seen in discussions of citizen duties: contributing socially and economically to their communities, aiding collective efforts, and standing shoulder-to-shoulder with the rest of the state. More importantly for my argument, they saw these actions as a reason to extend driving privileges. Thus, the carrying out of citizen duties—performing citizenship—triggered obligations on the part of the state; in this case, to allow undocumented residents to get driver authorization cards.

Policy Background

There are two federal policies that impact driver authorization cards. The first is the REAL ID Act of 2005 that requires states to comply with certain requirements when issuing driver's licenses. The guidelines require specific information to be included on the license (e.g., the individual's full legal name), a digital photo of the licensee, security features to prevent tampering, and mandates that certain documents (most notably, a social security card) are required prior to the issuance of a driver's license. As a result of the last requirement, states cannot allow noncitizens (i.e., those without a social security number) to obtain a driver's license. However, the state may provide a distinct category of card—typically called a driver authorization card—whose sole purpose is to establish that the bearer has passed the necessary tests and is allowed to drive. The card must be physically distinct from the state's driver's licenses and contain some form of verbiage that the card cannot be used for identification to ensure that the individual does not use the card to board an airplane (fears of terrorism) or vote (fears of usurping the voice of the demos).

The second federal action that impacts state-granted driver authorization cards is President Obama's executive action to defer deportations of those who arrived in the United States as children.

The Deferred Action for Childhood Arrivals program applies to those who arrived in the United States before they turned 16 and were under the age of 31 as of June 15, 2012. In addition, to qualify for DACA, the individual must have either completed high school or earned a GED and currently be attending school or serving in the military. Once this policy took effect, most states allowed those with a DACA ID to also obtain a driver's license, as the ID holder now had a form of federal identification. Due to these circumstances, and to avoid the "innocent child" argument seen in state-level DREAM Act debates, I look at states that extend the driving privilege to *all* undocumented members of their community, not just those with a DACA ID.

At the time of this writing, 13 states allow all undocumented residents to acquire a state-issued driver authorization card.[2] In order to explore the arguments used on either side of this issue, I gathered legislative transcripts—including written transcripts, videos, and audio files—covering roll call votes, floor debates, public hearings, and/or congressional meetings related to the prospective bills in all 13 states. I then identified patterns of arguments to uncover the major themes used by both opponents and proponents of the bills and to see whether different conceptions of citizenship emerged from the debates. Similar to state-level DREAM Acts, lawmakers disagreed on who was deemed part of the group to whom they owed consideration. That is, they differed as to whether they—as representatives of the state—owed obligations to undocumented residents. The determination of who was to be included, once again, had much to do with whether belonging was determined by nation-state authorization or if a more expansive notion of performing citizenship was considered.

Interestingly, Nebraska was initially one of only two states (the other being Arizona) that banned even those with a DACA ID from receiving this privilege. In 2015, the state legislature passed legislation that remedied this situation and, in so doing, extended the privilege to all residents. This expansion beyond DACA recipients resulted in Governor Ricketts (Republican) vetoing the bill. In a letter to the legislature explaining his decision, he called the policy an "unwarranted grant of an important state identification document to an overly broad group of illegal immigrants."[3] The legislature responded with a three-fifths majority vote to enact the bill notwithstanding the Governor's objections.

The Nebraska governor's concern about "an overly broad group" speaks to the differences between the discrete group of beneficiaries of tuition equity and the more general population of those able to get driver authorization cards under these new laws. These differences informatively allow us to re-examine the activities and characteristics of those to whom the state owes certain considerations. If the intended beneficiary is not an "innocent child," desert will be determined using a different metric. As we will see, and similar to debates surrounding tuition equity, a focus on actions and contributions—performing citizenship—will emerge as a powerful justification for extending driving privileges.

Right or Privilege?

One of the issues debated in regards to driver authorization cards is whether driving is a right or privilege. This is important because privileges are understood to be granted at the discretion of the person with the authority to bestow the privilege. In contrast, rights are understood—correctly or not—to be owed to those with a valid rights claim. Therefore, rights are much harder to deny than privileges. That being said, in order to have one's rights claim recognized as valid, one has to be seen as able to make that claim. As previously discussed, undocumented migrants are often denied the ability to claim rights against the nation-state in which they reside.

In terms of legislative debates on the issue, Representative Berrios (Democrat) went as far as to say that "[t]his Bill isn't a Latino issue or an undocumented issue. This is a human rights issue."[4] In this way, Representative Berrios bypasses the need for nation-state approval by arguing that individuals can claim the right based on merely being human. As previously discussed, evoking human rights may provide a certain level of moral persuasion, but has very little practical impact. For example, there are many rights listed in the United Nations Declaration of Human Rights, such as the right to rest and leisure, which the United States does not feel obligated to provide or protect. However, the rights of citizens are a different matter, and who counts as a citizen matters very much.

Nebraska, being the final state to extend driving privileges to DACA recipients, had the additional issue of justifying why it alone would not allow a benefit provided by every other state. During a public hearing about the proposed law, Adrian Sanchez, Lincoln-area representative of the Nebraska Latino American Commission, lamented that "Nebraska is the only state that does not recognize this fundamental legal right."[5] The assumption that driving is a fundamental legal right is as interesting as it is problematic. Many would argue that there is no such thing as a fundamental legal right. A greater number would argue that certain rights, such as the right to life and freedom from bodily harm, should be protected by any legitimate state authority. However, the idea that driving is similarly fundamental seems puzzling and unsubstantiated.

The speaker seems to rely on the fact that the other states have recognized the right; ergo, it must be a fundamental legal right. This opens the door to criticism. During the same hearing, Susan Gumm, self-identified merely as a citizen of Nebraska, argued that "[d]river's licenses are a privilege not a right, and noncitizens have no constitutional right to obtain a driver's license."[6] In truth, citizens do not have a constitutional right to drive either, as no such provision is provided in the United States Constitution. It is especially informative, though, that Ms. Gumm felt the need for the one-two punch. Driving is a privilege not a right, she argued. But even if it is a right, it is not one that should be granted to noncitizens. This recognizes the higher threshold of rights. That is, mere privileges can be denied with much less justification than can rights. In making the argument that undocumented individuals can be denied the right to drive because driving is a mere privilege, the underlying assumption is that if driving was a right, it may not be able to be denied. In turn, this rests on the assumption that perhaps undocumented members of our communities are owed some level of legal protections and rights.

In terms of this debate, whether driving is a right or privilege, there are more reasons to side with privilege. There are, for example, procedures to both grant and retract driving privileges. In addition, driving is not protected as a right in any enumerations of human or citizen rights of which I am aware. The fact, then, that undocumented residents are provided access to this privilege— a discretionary benefit—speaks even more strongly for the growing belief that they are owed more rights, protections, and entitlements than is currently recognized.

Rethinking Our Obligations

Similar to arguments used in state-level DREAM Acts, debates over driver authorization cards include discussions about the unfairness of immigration policies. That is, any fault lies with the federal government and its inability to enact a consistent and fair immigration policy. This method of framing placed the "illegal" act of residing without documents into a larger context and encouraged listeners to rethink what we might owe to undocumented members of our communities. Illinois Senator Raoul (Democrat), for instance, provided the following argument:

> A previous speaker talked about equitable application of our immigration laws. Let's not lie to ourselves—there's never been any such thing in this country. So, by fortuity, some people have legal immigration status in our country and some people don't. I can take you to the Haitian community in Florida and they can point to other communities that have—have gotten preferential treatment with regards to how our immigration laws are applied.[7]

Senator Raoul is referring to the preferential treatment given to Cuban migrants, one of many examples of United States immigration policies that are based on political, rather than economic or humanitarian, reasons.

Juan Gallegos, board member of the Nebraskans for Peace and a DACA recipient, described the personal impact of arbitrary immigration laws during a public hearing held by the Nebraska Transportation and Telecommunications Committee. "We have potential," he testified, "and we're always at the whim of somebody's pen."[8] In this, we see the call to focus on the person's contributions, to shift from paper citizenship to performing citizenship. Kathleen Erickson, a member of the Omaha Together One Community immigration action team, shared similar insights into changing immigration regimes and the role of businesses in soliciting migrant workers. Or, as she put it:

> Many of the immigrants I knew at that time had come to the United States because they had been encouraged, invited, or even recruited by businesses in the United States. . . . What happened was that the system changed. . . . The border changed very much and, as you know, our country changed very much after 9/11. So those people who had come to this country were raising their families and living ordinary lives and paying their taxes were caught in that system. . . . They have been criminalized and their families are being ripped apart in ways that they had no way to foresee.[9]

Such testimony encourages the audience to rethink issues of guilt and blame. Perhaps the guilty party is not the undocumented "lawbreaker," but the policy makers and business owners that have rigged the game and change the rules at the whim of their pen. Framing the discussion in this way, in turn, alters perceptions of the worthiness and desert of potential beneficiaries of the debated bills.

The failure of the federal government to fix the broken immigration system or pass comprehensive reform also allows the state room to act. That is, state lawmakers feel the need to address issues affecting undocumented residents because the federal government will not. Like the state-level DREAM Acts discussed in the prior chapter, state legislatures were not too concerned about entering the decidedly federal domain of immigration when debating driver authorization cards. Instead, these legislators felt emboldened to pass laws specifically impacting those individuals without federal legal status. During a floor debate in the Colorado House of Representatives, Representative Swalm (Republican) explained that he opposes the bill because he views it "as piecemeal immigration reform when we need comprehensive immigration reform."[10] To which Representative Melton (Democrat) responded that driver authorization cards were "a state issue, not a federal issue."[11] The federal government is still responsible for the larger immigration regime, but the state can help its residents through state-granted privileges.

Representative Melton's statement speaks to federalist views that states retain traditional state powers in such areas as policing and education. Thus, under federalism, state-granted identification can be seen as a traditional state function beyond the power of the federal government. However, it also implies that a policy directed at state residents is somehow a separate issue than that resident's immigration status. That is, a resident can be recognized by the state as a member of its community, regardless of whether the nation-state acknowledges that individual. In these ways, a space is provided for states to recognize and protect members of their community regardless of what the federal government does or does not do.

Lawmakers' recognition of the federal government's inability or unwillingness to address immigration concerns led to pragmatic arguments. A common argument used by proponents of driver authorization cards was that such legislation was just practical or merely an acknowledgement of reality. That is, people are already driving; if we admit it and pass this law, we can make sure they know the rules of the road and get insurance. Senator Brady (Republican), for example, framed the issue accordingly: "Fact of the matter is, they are not going to self-deport. The federal government's not going to deport them. They are here. We have to try to find some resolution to this."[12] Undocumented individuals, this argument goes, are in the state and they are driving. Pretending they are not—adopting the blindness of liberal theory—may be politically expedient but not realistic when dealing with real-world issues; in this case, the reality of people needing to drive but unable to be properly licensed or insured under existing state laws.

The same pragmatic approach was also occasionally used during debates about state-based DREAM Acts. For example, Senator Wehrbein (Republican), in defending the Nebraska tuition equity bill, claimed that "the landscape is changing in Nebraska. It's going to change a lot more in the future, and I think we have to recognize that and react accordingly. In other words, we've got to be realistic."[13] However, pragmatism was far more common when discussing driver authorization cards. Senator Cullerton (Democrat) argued that the bill was necessary and the "reason for this is we have perhaps a quarter of a million undocumenteds [sic] in the State of Illinois who are eligible—or, of driver's age. Many of whom, human nature being such as it is and the necessities of life being such as it is, are definitely driving."[14] Such a law, then, is not so much an extension of a privilege as it is a practical consideration.

Part of the reality lawmakers were asking their colleagues to accept was that the roads were currently unsafe due to drivers who are unlicensed and, therefore, probably uneducated about traffic laws and definitely uninsured. Oregon Senator Beyer (Democrat), for example, claimed the bill, "gets us to a realistic debate, a realistic position. . . . Doesn't allow them to get on an airplane, let's be clear about that. This is about driver safety."[15] In making pragmatic arguments, speakers linked undocumented migrants with unsafe highways and potentially other threats to the citizenry. Such threats were hinted at by Senator Beyer's assurance that card-bearers cannot get on an airplane and, assumedly, crash said airplane into the World Trade Center. The attention on the safety of the citizenry also shifts the focus away from privileges owed to undocumented members of the community to protections owed to the "real" citizens. For this reason, pragmatic arguments were problematic in that they set up an "us versus them" dynamic. Thus, similar to the "innocent child" argument in tuition-equity debates, an "othering" occurred even while arguing for the "other" to be included in the bestowal of a privilege.

To Whom the Obligation Is Owed: Protecting Citizens

The argument that the extension of driving privileges was necessary for highway safety was present in all states. Vermont Representative Donahue (Republican) succinctly summed up her position on this issue by simply stating: "I vote yes for safe driving."[16] Similarly, Senator Spearman (Democrat) explained "we are discussing protecting our citizens. I want to focus on this point. By ensuring people are fit to drive and are insured, we complement all other public safety policies we have."[17] The claim to highway safety rests on two major assumptions. First of all, that people will be safer drivers if they are required to pass written, driving, and vision tests. Secondly, that those currently driving without licenses will go through the process necessary once the option is open to them.

The first premise of the argument tended to lead to support of the bill. However, it had the unintended consequence of framing undocumented individuals as potential threats and problems to be solved. Senator Cullerton (Democrat) explained that his interest in the bill

> was really a selfish one for the citizens of the State of Illinois who are driving on our highways, who are being potentially jeopardized by so many undocumented folks who don't have a license, haven't been tested, might not know how to drive, might not have insurance. And from a selfish point of view, I think we should protect ourselves by asking them to get a license—by requiring them to get a license.[18]

In this formulation, documented citizens are the ones owed the state's protection. Undocumented residents receive a benefit merely as a means to an end. Senator Cullerton's formulation also explicitly sets up an "us versus them" framework with the call to protect "ourselves" by requiring "them" to comply. The second assumption, that people would willingly get licensed—follow the law—once they were able to, was met with skepticism. Such skepticism also opened the door for a larger discussion questioning whether those who violated immigration laws could *ever* be considered law-abiding members of society.

Senator Lundberg (Republican), who also moved to change the title of the bill to "Amnesty Act Part I," claimed that arguments about highway safety are flawed as people are going to drive anyway. In this way, he incorporated pragmatic arguments in defense of the bill (unlicensed drivers are already driving so we should allow them to get licenses), to argue against the bill (they are already driving without licenses and, not being law-abiding citizens, will continue to do so). He concluded that the bill, "will not make the roads safer—so if that's the argument you better move along and find a better argument."[19] Senator Kane (Republican) also questioned undocumented migrants' ability and willingness to follow the law.

> But, again, we've already stated that these individuals are already driving illegally. They're already driving without a license. They're already driving without insurance. They're already driving without—an unregistered car. What makes us think they're going to abide by the laws afterwards?[20]

Discussions of abiding or breaking the law not surprisingly led to the larger issue of entering the country without nation-state authorization and lawmakers' role in potentially condoning such actions. The California Transportation Committee's analysis of the proposed policy concluded: "The debate surrounding this issue is traditionally cast as trying to assure all motorists, whether citizens or not, are trained, tested, and insured versus the notion that licensing noncitizens will reward law breaking activity and encourage illegal immigration."[21] Instead of granting benefits, it is rewarding illegal behavior. Instead of extending privileges to members of our communities, it is protecting citizens against those individuals—in which case, what else do citizens need to be protected from?

The Menacing Other: Terrorism and Voter Fraud

The other major issue among bill opponents was a concern for domestic and national security and the potential abuses of a state-issued identification card. Senator Brady (Republican) explained his need to be assured that the driver authorization cards "cannot be used for identification purposes, which protects our security, I believe, from airports, the purchase of guns and ammunition, as well as the—- protects the right to vote."[22] Senator Boucher (Republican) raised the specter of terrorism once again. He warned that "[l]ooking back at the attacks of 9/11 and similar attacks, we ought to be very, very cautious."[23] Representative Kilmartin (Republican) first warns that the "bill expands drug cartel opportunities" and then continues with this dire prediction:

In addition to drug cartels, we need to understand terrorism. . . . we are putting mere convenience of those here illegally over the safety of our children and grandchildren . . . 'looking the other way' will not be an adequate answer to those who use the security loopholes in this bill to do us serious harm. It will do little to quell the tears and grief of the widow and her children when an act of terrorism causes the loss of a husband.[24]

The tradeoff Kilmartin presents of "mere convenience" on one side and the "safety of our children and grandchildren" is predicated on the belief that undocumented individuals, far from being members of our communities, intend to do us harm in all sorts of shadowy ways.

Another danger discussed was the threat to democratic legitimacy and popular sovereignty if newly-licensed undocumented residents used the state identification card to vote. Constant assurances were given that the card was different enough in appearance from real driver's licenses that no such voter fraud would take place. There was also some speculation about the rationality of a person that would risk instant deportation and lose any chance of attaining legal status in order to take part in a civic duty so few Americans engage in. During a discussion of potential voter fraud in Utah, Senator Davis (Democrat) pointed out that 40,000 ballots in the previous election had gone missing; what was described as an "inadvertent mistake," but what Senator Davis considered the "real concern" in terms of voter fraud.[25] However, many of Davis's colleagues did not see the concerns as comparable. The 40,000 lost ballots were portrayed more as an understandable—albeit problematic—consequence of mass democracy whereas a single vote by a noncitizen could undermine the legitimacy of the state. Representative Ramey (Republican) raised the issue of general identification fraud: "There are going to be far too many new people who will get these cards. There'll be fraud, abuse."[26] In these arguments we see the undocumented individual portrayed as a terrorist, a fraud, and usurper of the vote.

These images create the sense of the menacing other—someone from whom decent law-abiding citizens need protection. Vermont Representative Gage (Republican) concluded that "[o]ur safety as a nation is more important than giving driving rights to a few immigrant workers."[27] This sentiment sets up false trade-offs and exaggerates the threat while minimizing both the benefit derived by the policy as well as the deservingness of the proposed beneficiaries.

The division goes beyond distinctions based on legal status. It presumes demos-destroying activities based on the underlying logic that residing in the state without documents is the action of "them" not "us." The way to counter these arguments is through the discourse of inclusion in which undocumented residents should have the ability to drive legally; not because they currently pose a danger on the highways, but because they are members of our community. In this way, too, "who" the state is obligated to protect shifts from a subset of document-bearing citizens to the more general community of performing citizens.

Inclusive Arguments: Rethinking the "We"

The acknowledgement of shared membership in the community was more prevalent in the driver authorization debates than the DREAM Act debates. This may be due to the fact that DREAMers are a discrete category of young students—leading to arguments regarding why they are deserving (bright, ambitious, innocent, etc.). When dealing with the larger group of undocumented drivers, there is more of a necessity to make a claim for why they should be granted a privilege. Either it is a pragmatic policy to ensure highway safety, or the undocumented drivers are part of the community and deserving of the same privileges other community members can claim.

In making claims for inclusion, lawmakers made discursive moves similar to what we saw in the DREAM debates in which residents were referred to as, for example, "Nebraskans" or "our children" instead of "undocumented migrants" or the much more pejorative "illegal aliens." This change in labels signals inclusion, belonging and an intention of remaining. The individual is not in the process of migrating, they have planted roots in our state and are part of the amalgamated landscape. Senator Robles (Democrat), in making his case, flatly stated, "[u]ndocumented people in Nevada are part of the framework of Nevada."[28] Far from being other or secondary, they are at the very base of the state, providing support. Nebraskan Senator Nordquist (Democrat) similarly claimed "[t]hey're as much Nebraskan as I am." Vermont Representative Russel (Democrat) noted the "strong desire to fit into a community and state they have come to love. . . . We should embrace these newcomers as yet another one of the threads of our fabric. . . . My vote has been cast for inclusion."[29] The fabric of society—the threads combining into a beautiful tapestry—was a popular image and one that speaks to this notion of true imbrication into the community. All of these statements acknowledge that undocumented residents are already part of the community, acting like other state citizens, and therefore deserving of consideration and state-granted privileges. Once again, performing like a citizen is seen as an important justification for treating someone like a citizen.

The inclusive form of argument seems to have been successful. The states that relied more heavily on inclusive arguments—notably Nevada, Nebraska and Vermont—tended to have higher levels of support for the bills. At the same time, though, it is important to note that the bills passed with the highest margins of support in Georgia and Washington. Georgia is especially puzzling, as they overwhelmingly passed a law banning tuition equity for undocumented immigrants in 2008.[30] Given this, what could possibly explain Georgia's strong support for driver authorization cards? While the main purpose of the bill was to provide driving privileges to residents attempting to get their visas renewed, it did also allow authorization for those claiming they were going to seek asylum status as well as DACA recipients. Interestingly, the extension of the privilege to those with deferred status was barely mentioned and, in fact, not largely understood. The floor debates revealed a lack of knowledge about what was covered in the bill—including by those presenting it. Thus, it seems that the law's intent and impact were not recognized at the time it was passed.[31]

In the case of the Washington bill, discussions surrounding the proposal did not focus on the aspect of the bill that enabled undocumented residents to apply for "identicards." The Washington House Committee on Transportation held testimony for the bill. The issues covered during the hearings were "the use of illegally obtained driver's licenses in writing bad checks, the illegal use of credit cards, and the use of illegal driver's licenses as identification in underage drinking."[32] All recorded testimony was in support of the bill with no mention that undocumented residents would benefit. So while the bill had the result of supplying identicards to undocumented residents, that was a mere footnote to the larger purpose of bulking up identification requirements to ensure people were not obtaining state identification using false names or birthdates.

Aside from the strange cases of Georgia and Washington, inclusive arguments garnered the greatest support. I believe it was because they avoided the "othering" that resulted from arguments relying on highway safety. By replacing "us versus them" with just "us," inclusive arguments expanded the community of people that were owed consideration. Jan Gradwhol, a former judge, testified in front of the Nebraska State Transportation and Telecommunications Committee. She relied on inclusive arguments and concluded that there "is no reason for them to be singled out as a special group."[33] Thus, the argument is shifted away from special privileges being granted to a potentially undeserving group to part of the larger "we" being singled out in the denial of benefits. The burden of proof shifts from the individual to the state. If undocumented individuals are members of the social polity, the state is obligated to them in the same way it is to other "citizens." Once again, images of performing citizenship emerge, and those images provide an especially powerful rationale for triggering state-based obligations—both protections and privileges—to undocumented immigrants.

Performing Citizenship

During a floor debate in the Utah House of Representatives, Representative Litvack (Democrat) described the nation's handling of immigration as schizophrenic because the state benefits from the contributions made by migrants, but then turns around and tries to keep these same contributors from getting benefits. He concluded that this resulted in a creation of "second-class people that we are not treating them the same."[34] In his argument, we see both the concern of singling out members of the community and denying them benefits discussed above as well as an acknowledgement of undocumented residents' contribution to society. More importantly for my purposes, he links their contributions to the justified receipt of state benefits.

In a similar way, Representative Ure (Republican) links labor and the resulting contribution to the entitlement of certain privileges. He argued that "[w]e have a workforce here—that keeps our cost of living low—and we exploit them as labor. And I use that word very strongly and at the same time we have to have them here and we have to start to realize . . . that they have a privilege to drive."[35] Nebraska Senator Nordquist (Democrat) also notes contributions in the form of labor and wonders why the state would not encourage this contribution, or at least not block it. He asks his colleagues: "why would we want to limit their ability to work and to contribute to our economy?"[36] Senator Hardy (Republican) described undocumented drivers as shoulder-to-shoulder with other residents, but again relies on labor. He claimed "[t]he reality is they are here with us and working with and for us"[37] While recognition through labor is problematic—members of the community participate and give to their community in many ways other than wage labor—these arguments reveal a recognition of the contributions being made and an acknowledgement that they should continue (that is, not be blocked by the state's unwillingness to extend certain benefits).

Not everyone saw it this way, of course. There were those lawmakers who held to more traditional models of citizenship, in which only documents—not performances—can trigger state protections and privileges. They did not see the possibility that lawmakers could grant state recognition—or, at least, certain benefits—to members of their communities who were contributing in various ways. This idea, to them, undermined the larger legal structure and led to nonsensical results. Senator Jacobs (Democrat) questioned, "How do I, as a lawmaker, support a bill that gives undocumented workers the right to drive? Doesn't this, in effect, flout the law and make the law meaningless?"[38] Senator McLachlan (Republican) saw the involvement of the state as absurd: "If we look at a suggestion that a state government agency is going to issue a legal identification document to an individual who is undocumented, what is the Catch-22 there? What is the irony there? A legal document for an undocumented individual."[39] Within the framework of paper citizenship, recognition is limited to those with nation-state authorization. The idea of such an invisible being bearing state-granted identification without federal authorization is not only unthinkable, it is impossible. If citizenship is understood in this way, states have no ability to recognize their members outside of federally granted legal status.

Colorado Senator Lundberg (Republican) recognizes the claims being made; that is, that those performing citizenship should be entitled to certain benefits. He disagrees with this expanded understanding of citizenship and argues that "[i]t's purpose is to turn the whole legal process on its head and it's not going to make people legal."[40] Senator Lundberg's mindset—along with those who argue against the recognition of performing citizenship—firmly hold to conventional conceptions of nation-state citizenship and a specific understanding of the rule of law. Within this mindset, those without nation-state authorization fall outside of lawmakers' considerations. Obligation is only owed to paper citizens. Rights, much less discretionary privileges such as driving, should not be extended to unauthorized members of the community.

While these arguments mirror what many Americans believe, it should be noted that, in these cases, the opposition lost and access to driving privileges was extended to all members of the community.

Perhaps fear regarding highway safety carried the day. However, given the success of inclusive arguments based on performance-based citizenship, it seems likelier that an expansive notion of community membership, of who constitutes "us," resonated more deeply than an exclusive Westphalian notion of citizenship.

* * * * *

In this chapter, I have explored debates surrounding policies that allow undocumented residents access to driver authorization cards. Bill opponents used arguments that conjured up the image of a menacing other: unsafe driver, terrorist, and usurper of the vote. Framed in this way, undocumented residents were not seen as members of the community but a threat to the citizenry. Consequently, there was no obligation owed to noncitizens. The duty of the state was limited to the protection of paper citizens.

Some supporters of the policy based their arguments on the practical results of increasing highway safety by ensuring all drivers were licensed and insured. However, this line of reasoning played right into the image of the undocumented individual as a threat from which the citizenry needed protection. This argument was similar to the "innocent child" defense of state-level DREAM Acts. In both cases, what appears to be a pragmatic political strategy to garner support has the unintended consequence of setting up problematic dichotomies. Arguments framed in this way present members of the undocumented community—be that parents of DREAMers or unlicensed drivers—as other; that is, not us. It is then only a small step to making the claim that such outsiders are not owed obligations on the part of the state, be that rights or privileges.

Similar to what we saw with tuition equity debates, the most successful arguments supporting driver authorization cards were those that incorporated inclusive language and relied on images of a cohesive community. The power behind these inclusive arguments is that they also provided a picture of performing citizenship. Those who work with us, live with us, and contribute both socially and economically *are* us. It is through these behaviors, these performances, that they earn inclusion into the group of people that have earned the right to equal consideration.

As I have argued throughout the book, altering our frame of reference to an inclusive, performance-based standard of citizenship also shifts the obligations owed. Within this new framework, the state now owes obligations to those performing citizenship. That is, by performing civic duties, undocumented residents trigger certain state protections and entitlements. Once undocumented residents are included in the community of those considered, the obligations on the part of the state—instead of protecting the "real" citizens from the menacing other—extend to all those performing citizenship. Thus, the *who*, *what*, and *why* of political obligation is altered. As seen through legislative debates, the *who* becomes the state, the *what* is driver authorization cards, and the *why* is because undocumented residents carry out civic duties—perform citizenship—in ways indistinguishable from paper citizens.

Notes

1 Vermont State House of Representatives floor debate, May 7, 2013.
2 California, Colorado, Connecticut, Georgia, Illinois, Maryland, Nebraska, Nevada, New Mexico, Oregon, Utah, Vermont, and Washington. Percentage of support for the bills by state and chamber can be found in Appendix A.
3 Nebraska Legislative Journal (Eighty-Eighth Day—May 29, 2015), p. 1909–1910.
4 Illinois State House of Representatives floor debate transcripts for January 8, 2013, 46.
5 Nebraska State Transportation and Telecommunications Committee public hearing, March 3, 2015.
6 Nebraska State Transportation and Telecommunications Committee public hearing, March 3, 2015.
7 Illinois State Senate transcript for December 4, 2012, 46.
8 Nebraska State Transportation and Telecommunications Committee public hearing transcripts for March 3, 2015.
9 Ibid.
10 Colorado State House of Representatives floor debate, April 29, 2013.
11 Ibid.
12 Illinois Senate transcript, December 4, 2012, 26.
13 Nebraska Legislature transcripts, March 29, 2006, 12059.
14 Illinois Senate transcript, December 4, 2012, 22.
15 Oregon State Senate floor debate, April 23, 2013.
16 Vermont State House of Representatives floor debate, May 7, 2013.
17 Nevada Senate transcripts, April 3, 2013, 19.
18 Illinois Senate transcript, December 4, 2012, 41–2.
19 Colorado State Senate floor debate, April 25, 2013.
20 Connecticut State Senate transcript for May 29, 2013, 60.
21 Bill Analysis of AB60 by the California Transportation Committee, 9/12/2013, p. 4.
22 Illinois State Senate transcript for December 4, 2012, 27.
23 Connecticut State Senate transcript for May 29, 2013, 21.
24 Vermont State House of Representatives floor debate, May 7, 2013.
25 Utah State Senate floor debate, February 18, 2005.
26 Illinois State House of Representatives transcripts for January 8, 2013, 42.

27 Vermont State House of Representatives floor debate, May 7, 2013.
28 Nevada State Senate transcripts for April, 3, 2013, 18.
29 Vermont State House of Representatives floor debate, May 7, 2013.
30 In fact, this law banning tuition equity garnered 98% support in the Senate and 100% support in the House of Representatives.
31 The Georgia floor debates are videotaped and provide a rather riveting view of state law making. In both houses, the bill was sponsored by freshman legislators—their very first bill in both cases. This was clearly a rite of passage and most of the questions involved various forms of ribbing. Questions included asking the sponsor in the Senate, Senator Hill (Republican) to sing the West Point war chant. The sponsor in the House, Representative Demetrius (Democrat), was asked what position he played while on the University of Georgia football team. Only one Senator raised the question regarding asylum seekers as well as asking for a definition of "deferred action status." The author of the bill thought asylum referred to mental institutions and admitted he did not know what deferred action meant. This led Senator Kennedy (Republican) to proclaim, "It sounds like a good way of breaking the law." However, this must not have given him pause as the bill passed with 100% support from the senate. Likewise, the House of Representatives passed the bill with 99% of the chamber voting in favor.
32 House Bill Report for HB 1444, 4/20/1993.
33 Nebraska State Transportation and Telecommunications Committee hearing transcripts for March 3, 2015.
34 Utah State House of Representatives floor debate, February 22, 2005.
35 Utah State House of Representatives floor debate, February 22, 2005.
36 Nebraska State Transportation and Telecommunications Committee public hearing, March 3, 2015.
37 Nevada Assembly Committee on Transportation transcripts for May 25, 2013, 11.
38 Illinois State Senate floor debate transcripts for December 4, 2012, 41.
39 Connecticut State Senate floor debate transcript for May 29, 2013, 25.
40 Colorado State Senate floor debate, April 25, 2013.

6   Conclusion

I hope that one day we can all come to terms and see that we're not really different because you never know where there are DREAMers or there are DACA recipients in your life. We are everywhere in every facet of your life. You may just not see it.

—Fatima Flores-Lagunas, DACA recipient and Omaha resident[1]

Ms. Flores-Lagunas, in the above epigraph, voices the frustration of being viewed as "other," if being seen at all. This speaks to the limitations of a liberal theory of citizenship and the resulting liberal democracies that only recognize those individuals who have been authorized by the nation-state. The failure to see or hear all members of our communities has led to a limited group of people to whom the state believes it has obligations. Yet, this narrow understanding of citizenship is being actively contested in theory, in public discourse, and in state legislatures. Increasingly, people are calling for a new conception of citizenship that recognizes more than state-issued documents.

As seen throughout the book, a promising route to a more expanded notion of citizenship is to focus on the actions of community members. Those who are engaged in a common life, contribute both socially and economically, and have a sense of shared fate with the community—those performing citizenship—should be recognized as members of the polis. Undocumented members of our communities are often similarly situated to their neighbors in every way but papers. As Ms. Flores-Lagunas reminds us, as a DACA recipient and Omaha resident, she is "not really different" from other Nebraskan residents. As such, she is deserving of the same rights and protections granted other citizens. A performance-based conception of citizenship would acknowledge her contributions and provide her recognition.

The Impact of Reconceptualizing Citizenship

Citizenship is a crucial concept. As such, it should not be jettisoned, but reframed. United States citizenship provides rights and protections that grant security beyond what can be expected from human rights claims. Similarly, theories of moral obligation have not translated into actual protections for those vulnerable due to their legal status. Without a political component that can grant protections, recognition, and voice, undocumented members of our communities are left in the shadows. Therefore, a new conception of citizenship is necessary.

Senator Markley (Republican), in his opposition to extending driving privileges to undocumented residents, explained:

> I oppose this legislation because I believe firmly in the essential importance of citizenship, and I believe there's no other ground on which we can meet but as citizens of the United States. As citizens we're equal. We stand on the same principles. We stand devoted to the same flag. We are subject to the same laws, and we are entitled to the same rights and the same protections.[2]

Many would agree with this sentiment—depending on how you define citizen. Undocumented members of our communities are subject to the same laws, devoted to the same flag, and stand on the same principles. However, exactly because the current understanding of citizenship is limited by nation-state authorization, they do not have equal rights and protections. The logic of this distinction is being questioned as conceptions of citizenship are increasingly contested and expanded.

As I have argued throughout the book, a shift in conventional conceptions of political obligation can provide a theoretical grounding for a new form of citizenship. In its most basic understanding, political obligation is understood as a justification for why citizens are obligated to carry out certain civic duties—such as paying taxes or joining the military. These obligations are generated as a result of the goods the state provides its citizens. I argue that instead of individuals being obligated to the state because of the goods provided, the state should become obligated to provide goods to those who are carrying out their civic duties and contributing to the community—that is, those performing citizenship. Instead of the conferral of state's rights triggering an obligation on the part of the individual, the acting out of civic duties should trigger the corollary rights and protections owed to citizens.

If such a shift were to occur in our understandings of citizenship, the group to whom we owe obligations and equal consideration would increase to include undocumented residents who are engaged in a shared life with the community. Performing citizenship would determine paper citizenship. The type of performance that would trigger state obligations needs to come from a rooted position, be sustained over time, and provide contributions to the larger social scheme. That is, the individual must be imbricated into their community and have a sense of shared fate—the notion of standing shoulder to shoulder we have seen employed by many of the state legislators during the debates discussed in the book. Once this has been achieved, those performing citizenship deserve the rights and protections granted other citizens.

Public debates over the extensions of benefits and privileges give us insight into the concerns and contradictions our current situation engenders. We see how constructed images lead to determinations about who is deserving of certain benefits—and who is not. More importantly, we also see when groups are included in the "we"—creating collective intention that can form the basis of a new type of citizenship. It is clear that traditional conceptions of citizenship are evolving as lawmakers take into account more than just nation-state authorization. If states continue to recognize those performing citizenship, and see such performances as generating obligations on the part of the state, there will be serious policy implications.

Policy Implications

As seen in this book, an expanded notion of citizenship had real results when it came to successfully arguing for in-state tuition rates and driving privileges for undocumented residents. Once a different metric was used to determine desert—that is, actions and contributions instead of state-granted legal status—the group of deserving beneficiaries grew. This was limited to 20 states for tuition equity bills and 13 for driver authorization cards. However, proposals in other states are being introduced. Also, arguments are being made for other rights and privileges. For example, five states have now allowed undocumented college students to apply for state financial aid. This number will certainly grow in the coming years. There have also been proposals for other rights, including attempts to extend voting rights to noncitizens.

In much of the United States' history, the right to vote was not limited to citizens. From the founding until 1926, "22 states and federal territories allowed noncitizens to vote in local, state, and even federal elections" (Hayduck and Wucker 2004). These laws were gradually repealed, largely as a result of anti-immigrant sentiment. Recently, however, several cities have passed laws or ordinances allowing noncitizens to vote in local elections and/or school board elections. Proponents argue that all community members should have a voice in the laws to which they are subject, especially those involving their immediate communities and their children's education. Another argument is that it allows noncitizens to engage in a local form of citizenship which aids in the assimilation process if and when they become United States citizens. In this, we see a recognition of local citizenship as separate but related to nation-state citizenship. It also reveals the acknowledgment that community engagement and belonging should lead to those members' voices being heard and recognized.

In 2014, New York State lawmakers proposed the most sweeping attempt to grant state citizenship. The "New York is Home Act," if passed, would allow undocumented residents that have lived and paid taxes in New York for at least three years the right to run for office and vote in state and local elections. In addition, state citizens would qualify for Medicaid, financial aid, driving privileges, and professional licensing. Theodore Ruthizer, an immigration law professor at Columbia Law School, declared it a "horrible idea," adding that "citizenship should not be watered down and should not be rendered meaningless" (Eidelson 2014). In contrast, Peter Markowitz, a law professor at the Cardozo School of Law, claimed the act is "exercising a firmly established, constitutionally enshrined authority of the state to determine the boundaries of its own political community . . . New York gets to decide who are New Yorkers" (Eidelson 2014).

Here again we see an example of drastically different conceptions of citizenship. If citizenship is based on nation-state authorization, the extension of any citizen benefits or rights to those without papers is undermining the very meaning of citizenship. Conversely, if the meaning of citizenship involves community belonging and active engagement, it makes perfect sense for the state to recognize its own membership and to confer both benefits and political access accordingly. Once an individual is recognized as a member of a shared community, the state owes them equal consideration. In this, we see both the inclusive nature of a performance-based citizenship and the ability to use this conception of citizenship as a way to generate state obligations owed to all members of the community.

Steps Forward

State and local governments have started to adopt policy proposals that extend rights, protections, and privileges to undocumented residents. This speaks to an expanded notion of membership that is not predicated on nation-state citizenship. However, assuming that the federal government does not pass comprehensive immigration reform, we will continue to see fights over tuition equity, driving, voting, access to financial aid, and other privileges and protections. Regardless of the outcome, these contentious policies will continue to question, contest, and potentially reformulate our conceptions of citizenship.

One implication drawn from the research presented in this book is that inclusive arguments—those that refer to the individuals who would be impacted by the proposed policies as, for example, *our* community members or merely Nebraskans—are the most effective at garnering support for policies that extend benefits to undocumented residents. This is partially due to the fact that arguments based on inclusion avoid the "us versus them" divide that can occur when the proposed beneficiaries are singled out in any way—even when done so to make a claim for their innocence and merit. Thus, such arguments shift the focus from differences (legal status) to similarities (Americans in every way but on paper). But the success of the arguments also relied on a new conception of citizenship—in which belonging was determined by involvement in the community, not documents—resonated with people. By recognizing the actions of the individuals—paying taxes and contributing to the community in a variety of ways—lawmakers acknowledged that certain benefits were owed as a result. That is, performing citizenship triggered obligations on the part of the state to extend certain rights and privileges to those individuals, regardless of nation-state authorization.

As I have argued throughout the book, flipping our understandings of political obligation will expand the group to whom obligations are owed. Those who perform citizenship should be recognized as members of the polis and granted the corresponding rights and protections. Far from watering down citizenship, this will imbue it with new meaning. Instead of being based on state-issued papers, political membership should be granted to those who contribute to—and are engaged in—the community; those with common interests and a sense of shared fate. In short, a performance-based citizenship would merely recognize that those standing shoulder to shoulder with us already are Americans.

Notes

1 Nebraska State Transportation and Telecommunications Committee public hearings, March 3, 2015.
2 Connecticut State Senate transcript for May, 29, 2013, 79.

References

Eidelson, Josh. 2014. "New York State Mulls Citizenship for Undocumented Workers." *Bloomberg Businessweek,* June 16, 2014. Accessed June 16, 2014: http://www.businessweek.com/articles/2014-06-16/
Hayduk, Ron and Michele Wucker. 2004. "Immigrant Voting Rights Receive More Attention." *Migration Policy*, November 1, 2004. Accessed August 19, 2015: http://www.migrationpolicy.org/print/4725#.Vf3O-JZfSLow

Appendix A
Percentage of Support for State-Level Bills

			DREAM Acts			Driving Authorization Cards		
					% in Favor			% in Favor
Midwest	Illinois	House	2003	D	96%	2012	D	59%
		Senate		D	98%		D	73%
	Kansas	House	2004	R	56%			
		Senate		R	63%			
	Minnesota	House	2013	D	58%			
		Senate		D	62%			
	Nebraska	Unicameral	2006	R	55%	2015	R	77%
Northeast	Connecticut	House	2011	D	55%	2013	D	57%
		Senate		D	60%		D	54%
	New Jersey	Assembly	2013	D	59%			
		Senate		D	68%			
	New York	Assembly	2002	R	52%			
		Senate		D	72%			
	Vermont	House				2013	D	73%
		Assembly					D	93%

South								
South	Florida	House	2014	R	72%			
		Senate		R	65%			
	Georgia	House				2013	R	99%
		Senate					R	100%
	Maryland	House	2011	D	59%	2013	D	62%
		Senate		D	53%		D	60%
	Texas	House	2001	R	99%			
		Senate		R	90%			

West								
West	California	Assembly	2001	D	79%	2013	D	72%
		Senate		D	79%		D	78%
	Colorado	House	2013	D	66%	2013	D	52%
		Senate		D	66%		D	57%
	Nevada	Assembly				2013	D	71%
		Senate					D	95%
	New Mexico	House	2005	D	61%	2003	D	65%
		Senate		D	90%		D	59%
	Oregon	House	2013	D	68%	2013	D	66%
		Senate		D	63%		D	74%
	Utah	House	2002	R	53%	2005	R	75%
		Senate		R	77%		R	72%
	Washington	House	2003	R	79%	1993	D	100%
		Senate		D	100%		D	100%

Note: The Political Party controlling the legislature is indicated with a D for Democrat and R for Republican.

Index

For Product Safety Concerns and Information please contact our EU
representative GPSR@taylorandfrancis.com
Taylor & Francis Verlag GmbH, Kaufingerstraße 24, 80331 München, Germany

www.ingramcontent.com/pod-product-compliance
Ingram Content Group UK Ltd.
Pitfield, Milton Keynes, MK11 3LW, UK
UKHW021421080625
459435UK00011B/107